KING to KING
Preventing Generational Annihilation

Bishop Willie Bolden

KING to KING
Preventing Generational Annihilation

Bishop Willie Bolden

Copyright © 2014 by Bishop Willie Bolden

All rights reserved. No part of this publication may be reproduced, stored in a retrieval system, or transmitted, in any form or by any means, electronic, mechanical, photocopying, recording, or otherwise, without the prior written permission of the publisher.

Printed in the United States of America.
The information contained in this book is for educational purposes and not for diagnosis, prescription, or treatment of any kind whatsoever. This information should not replace consultation with a competent professional. The author and publisher are in no way liable for any misuse of the material. This publication contains the opinions and ideas of its author. It is to provide helpful and informative material on the subject matter covered.

First Printing: November 2014

Library of Congress Cataloging-in-Publication Data
Bolden, Willie

KING to KING: Preventing Generational Annihilation

Bishop Willie Bolden
ISBN 978-0-6922-4447-0

1. Religion 2. Leadership

Book design: iVue Graphics and Media Solutions

Editing Services Cee Cee Caldwell-Miller of Diamond Enterprises, Int'l

Dedication

I dedicate this first book to the Glory of God who inspired and helped me write it.

To my Parents Rev. Willie and Erma Bolden who started me on this journey of loving and serving the Lord whom they loved and served dearly.

Acknowledgements

To my son Jonathan and his wife Krystal who helped me with the art and production of this book.

To Roberta Barnes for her love and support.

To all of those who helped with the finances to bring this book to fruition, especially to Pastor Eugene and Myrtis Stevenson.

To the men that mentored me Pastor John Lloyd, the late Dr. Paul E. Paino and the late Archbishop Benson Andrew Idahosa.

Table of Contents

Foreword

Introduction: King to King- Mentoring in the Kingdom

Chapter One: Mentorship	12
Chapter Two: Instructions for a Future King	18
Chapter Three: The Kingdom Operates Under Covenant	25
Chapter Four: Walking in agreement with the King	38
Chapter Five: Steps to Kingdom Success	41
Chapter Six: God's Method was a Sign	56
Chapter Seven: Breaking Curses	69
Chapter Eight: Building Successfully	86
Chapter Nine: Monitor Your Heart Condition	100
Chapter Ten: Evil and your Destiny	116
Chapter Eleven: Closing the door of Offense	125
Chapter Twelve: Reaching the Family	138
Chapter Thirteen: The Woman Under Attack	156
Chapter Fourteen: The Child	167
Chapter Fifteen: Time and Attitude	178
About the Author	192

Foreword

Every generation has to wrestle with both God and His Word and do the "work" of theology. It is not simply the work of scholars; it is the work of every person, young and old who follows Jesus. The current culture is one in which there are "no absolutes" (which ironically, the statement itself is an absolute). Yet, the opportunity for the absolute truth of Jesus, who is the truth, and who sent His very own Spirit of Truth is engaging the culture at every level, and often in places where the institutionalized church has refused to engage, is perhaps greater than ever. My dear friend, Bishop Willie Bolden, a seasoned trans-generational voice in the Kingdom invites us in this work to see again through new eyes what God is doing across the generational boundaries, and remember who it is we serve and what it is He has called us to be, to do, and to obtain!

As we move forward into the 21st Century, the art and skill of "leading from behind" is going to become paramount for all who are involved at any level of mentor-coaching, if we are to prevent what Bishop Bolden calls "Generational Annihilation". Take time as you read through this treatise on the nature of kingship and apostolic reproduction from a perspective of Christ's Kingdom. It will be well worth your investment and critical thinking skills.

Bishop Mark J. Chironna, MA, PhD
Mark Chironna Ministries
Church On The Living Edge
Orlando, Florida

Introduction
King to King- Mentoring in the Kingdom

I was born again during a time called the Jesus movement. This was one of the most rebellious times that America has ever faced. There were protest to the Vietnam War. Open protest in the streets over almost anything you can think of. We protested in our music, one was so overwhelmed that he asked What's Going on. We openly attacked the office of the Presidency and the president broke into buildings. Many of us thought drugs were the answer, if we could put drugs in the water system there would be peace in the world. We had racial tension that some people put together organizations to protect ourselves from the others. Whole neighborhoods were bombed to stop these movements. We had groups in California killing people and writing messages in blood on the wall. We had outdoor concerts that were an open orgy and drug fest. I want us to remember a war we were in that we never won. Yet so many young people lost their lives in the defense of this country, only yet to come home and have someone spit in their face for putting their life on the line. This war also caused people to lose careers and families to avoid participating in something they did not believe in. There was drug dealing and prostitution on a large scale; it was such a part of our cultural, there were movies that glorified this behavior.

I wanted us to take a trip down memory lane because we sometimes think reaching this generation for Christ is an impossible task. Yet, in this past generation, God raised up men and women that would turn a lot of that generation to Him. I will highlight a few. Men like Oral Roberts had a Christian University to develop people lives. Men like Dr. Fredrick K.C. Price filled auditoriums and taught young people to walk by faith. Who could forget the work of Dr. Billy Graham and the Evangelistic outreaches he had. There were groups like Andréa Crouch, who were innovators in Gospel music along with Nancy Honeytree, Phil Driscol, and many other pioneers to turn young people's heart to God.

These people did not take the comfortable road and stick with the status quo, but thought outside the proverbial box, and with the help of the spirit was very creative in their approach.

    There was a Pastor by the name of Dr. Paul E. Paino, in Fort Wayne Indiana, that so many people persecuted for his approach to reaching young people. As if this mattered, I am a black man and remember while in the world lost how this church got my attention. I would pass this church sometimes high on drugs and can still remember my thoughts as I passed by. They were running more buses than the city and I would say, "If I were to go to church it would be one like that one" and I would always finish with the devil reminding me that I was black and would not be welcomed there. This was not the case at all. This church was determined to make an impact in their community so there was a youth ministry developed. The youth ministry was ran by another innovator by the name of John Lloyd, he started a coffee house called the Adams Apple, I would venture to say that thousands of young and not so young people were converted at the Adams Apple, I being one of them. I still cry when I am in his presence because I know if he had not obeyed God I would be lost.

    I divert a little to tell my story. John and the young people he had reached most by going down town with a real rock band playing at first secular music and then John would give a salvation message. This was the approach at first and then it changed as these young people matured and desired to praise God with music that honored Him. I wandered in one night to a place I thought was a nightclub thinking I was going to a secular concert. Not only was it not a secular concert but I got the wrong night and walked into a concert. I was involved in drugs and prostitution and by that pulled into the occult. When I went in, I thought I was as spiritual as they were and took them up on it. To my surprise, these young people were serious about God and his presence was evident. God spoke to me in an audible voice and said this was his doing and it was my last opportunity, it was there I received Christ on a Wednesday night. Thursday I went to the church for Bible study, Friday I came to the concert I was looking for the first night, Saturday prayer meeting, church all day Sunday and Monday I enrolled in Bible College. They also knew how to pray, they were reaching whites and some Latinos but no blacks and were praying to reach that community also God used me to go in that community and thousands came to Christ and answered their prayers.

Dr. Paino suffered criticism for allowing people like me and long -haired smelling people called hippies to be a part of the church. Some of us suffered at the hands of those who disagreed with his methods. One time. I during communion, an Elder would turn his back to keep from looking me in my face. There were the racial jokes made, I did not feel welcomed at all. There was open criticism toward him and his family for coming outside the norm. What happened doing this time is that people fell on their faces, for God to give them Holy ideas to reach a generation that was hell bound and God answered their prayers.

We must not give up on this generation even though it is quite different from our generation. They do not think, feel or even believe as we do. Programmed by a group of educators hell bent on removing God from this society and they are doing a good job at it. Sin is no sin but situational. Truth is no longer truth but your truth. Time separated into sound bites. The music is no longer that but beats. The lyrics degraded an accepting female audience. Being a murderer helps you sale more CD's. Respect and honor are from a time gone by. Fathers do not have time for their children and mothers lives far out way the needs and life of a child. Yet knowing all of this, God has given us the task of reaching this generation with everything we have in us.

Chapter One
Mentorship
Knowing who you are and who they are.

Knowing who we are and who they are will help us with the mission of reaching the next generation in mentorship.

Genesis 1: [26] *Then God said, "Let us make mankind in our image, in our likeness, so that they may rule over the fish in the sea and the birds in the sky, over the livestock and all the wild animals,* [a] *and over all the creatures that move along the ground."*

It is impossible to reach this next generation without knowing who we are and who they are. In the very beginning, God designed man to have authority on the earth. When God made man, he made man in his image. It is necessary to note that he made man both male and female. Therefore, when we talk of man we are not talking gender. He gave man authority on the earth. However, there is something auspiciously missing from the list that man has authority over. The thing that is missing is another man. Every man is a King. That means that submission to another is an act of humility. Submission is the yielding of one King to another to accomplish a common goal. We must point this next generation into their Kingship. Remember when we study the scripture that said Jesus thought it not robbery to be equal with God but made himself of no reputation and humbled himself even to the death on the cross. The emphasis should be placed on the fact that he made himself of no reputation but humbled himself. We humble ourselves because it is the will of God concerning us and it will be good for our benefit. Notice God places people over us and then asks us to submit to them. We submit to leadership of others for a few reasons. Number one God made us, the King and is our direct authority. Being direct authority, he can place someone over us, which becomes indirect authority. Because God being our direct authority placed them there, it is he himself that we respond to. The next reason is that man has authority on the earth given by God. Man also has the ability to bless others. Obey them that have the rule over you for they watch for your soul that they may do it with joy and not with grief because that would be unprofitable for you. There is an additional profit in submitting in the Kingdom.

Let us look at a very important scripture, *3 John 1: ² "Beloved, I wish above all things that thou mayest prosper and be in health, even as thy soul prospeth."* I want you to notice God's desire for us is health and prosperity. Also, notice that health and wealth are attached to the soul and not the spirit man. This is related to the one responsible for your soul and that is your spiritual leader. To the same degree that I submit myself to learn from my leader, then I will be blessed. I will also venture to say that if I submit to my leader then whatever is under me in the Kingdom will submit to me. The opposite is also true, if I rebel then that which is under me will rebel. Remember we reap what we have sown.

Let us examine another passage that shows how God views us. *Psalm 8: ³ When I consider your heavens, the work of your fingers, the moon and the stars, which you have set in place, ⁴ what is mankind that you are mindful of them, human beings that you care for them?[c] ⁵ You have made them[d] a little lower than the angels[e] and crowned them[f] with glory and honor. ⁶ You made them rulers over the works of your hands; you put everything under their[g] feet: ⁷ all flocks and herds, and the animals of the wild, ⁸ the birds in the sky, and the fish in the sea, all that swim the paths of the seas.*

There is a powerful question that is asked of God after this strong statement. Let us look at the statement first. The speaker has observed the universe God has created in its entirety and its splendor and is in awe. Then he compares it to another of God's creation, which leaves a question in his mind. Look at what made him ask this question. Man with the naked eye can see five thousand stars. With a four-inch telescope, it would increase to two million and in one of the large observatories that number would jump to a billion. They say it would take you forty billion years to travel the universe at the speed of light. That is a vast amount of space.

With all that God has created, this little creature called man, seems to be his greatest creation. So a question arises in the heart of the speaker. Who is man? First, he is amazed that God constantly has man on his mind. When you look at the other parts of creation in their obedience to God and man being rebellious, why is God thinking about man? Yet he is, for he says he does not count slackness as man does but he is hoping man will change his mind and return to him. It is one thing to have this rebellious creature on his mind, but he also visits and cares for man. God spends his time thinking and caring for this rebellious creature. We should all repent when we hear what God said through the prophet Jeremiah. Jeremiah 29: [11] "For I know the plans I have for you, declares the LORD, plans to prosper you and not to harm you, plans to give you hope and a future." Everything a house, a boat, television, telephone, the internet all started with a plan and the inventor knew the purpose of his invention. God reminds us that we too started with a plan. The plan was a good one not to destroy you but to prosper you. Most of us are living outside that plan and struggling. The only way a thing finds its purpose is to know the heart of the inventor or creator. It is in the mind and heart of our creator the plans he has for us. This next generation must know that they are not an accident or a freak of nature. It does not matter if your parents did not even want you, you did not surprise God.

In this plan, God is optimistic for you in Psalm 8 he talks of your creation and that he explains your purpose. He said he made you a little lower than the Angels. First, let us look at this. The word Angel here is not the word normally translated Angel. Nevertheless, it is the word Elohim, the plural name for God himself. So God is saying he made you just a little lower than himself. That should tell you what God thought of you right from the beginning. You are to be like him and be a King or god little "g" on the earth. We sing a song in the church that most of us just sing and not believe. The song tells us that we have his love his power and his ability. If this is true, why don't we see it demonstrated? I have already mentioned that this generation must have an experience.

Our Churches must be a place where his love, his power and his ability must be experience by this generation of congregants. That would have been awesome all by itself but God goes further and says that he crowned you. Royalty is the only thing crowned. The Apostle Peter states in *1 Peter 2:* [9] *"But you are a chosen people, a royal priesthood, a holy nation, God's special possession, that you may declare the praises of him who called you out of darkness into his wonderful light.* [10] *Once you were not a people, but now you are the people of God; once you had not received mercy, but now you have received mercy."*

You were chosen to be royalty, but are you operating as a royal one. Some time ago, a baby was born in England and everyone was excited about his arrival. Newspaper reporters and other media camped out for weeks to report his coming. Once he was born a process that was not before the cameras began, that is the process of training him to be a royal. There are things you do not know just because you were born to be a royal. When you were born, again in the Kingdom of God you were to be a royal. Therefore, you need to be train so you do not embarrass the King who made you King. In Psalm 8, the crown was to bring glory and honor. Some royals act more like jackasses, we have seen some from Britain come to America and embarrass the throne. We have seen plenty that are a part of the Kingdom of God, yet they embarrass the King with their lifestyle and actions.

The Bible says let us walk worthy of our calling. We are

to follow the author and finisher of our faith. When you bring shame, it not only affects you but all citizens of the Kingdom. You are a King and will raise up other Kings. When you are working with the next generation are you developing Kings or slaves? Let us develop Kings.

Attributes of the King

We will look at the life of a King in the Old Testament that God said was a man after his own heart. If you are not trying to please the one who made you King then you are wasting your time. David was not just after the hand of God but wanted to know God's heart. Knowing God's heart will assure you of making the right decision in your rule. David said God your word I have hidden in my heart that I might not sin against thee. When you know God's heart, you also know what to tell others to help them get through. Knowing the heart of God, you will not be deceived by the enemy. How many times when we fall we thought to ourselves that God no longer loves us. Because we know his heart, we know it is a lie. When we face sickness the devil tells us we are going to die. We know the heart of God, we claim and stand in our healing. When we know the heart of God, we do not stop because we have opposition. Listen to David in the 23 Psalms.

> *Psalm 23: "The LORD is my shepherd, I lack nothing. [2] He makes me lie down in green pastures, he leads me beside quiet waters, [3] he refreshes my soul. He guides me along the right paths for his name's sake. [4] Eventhough I walk through the darkest valley, [a] I will fear no evil, for you are with me; your rod and your staff, they comfort me. [5] You prepare a table before me in the presence of my enemies. You anoint my head with oil; my cup overflows. [6] Surely, your goodness and love will follow me all the days of my life, and I will dwell in the house of the LORD forever."*

Even though David would be a King, he recognized

the Kingship of the Lord. He understood God to be the remover of that which is lacking in his house. This is Kingship Training 101; you must know God as a provider and instill it in your mentee. He will lead you to that which satisfies. David saw himself as a sheep and green pasture and still waters are necessary for sheep. We will be led places that will seem to consume us. If we remember you did not get here by yourself you were led here, your fears will soon dissipate at the knowledge of his presence. When I am off course, he will comfort me by not allowing me to self-destruct. He knows in my determination to eat I do not sometime see the danger so he goes ahead of me and prepare the table by removing what I should not eat and also those enemies that would destroy me. It is his anointing that protects me when I stick my nose where it should not be. Shepherds sometimes place heavy oil on the face of the sheep to protect it from serpents. God wants us to have more than enough for every good cause. We need to practice the presence of God to know he will always be with us. We also need to put emphasis on the importance of God's house. Notice the humility of David to compare himself not to something lofty but to a lowly sheep. How many sheep have you seen in a circus act? I would venture to say not many because sheep are one of the dumbest animals. They have to be taught repeatedly.

Chapter Two
Instructions for a Future King

I want us now to take a look at David training Solomon. We begin in *1 Kings 2:1 When the time drew near for David to die, he gave a charge to Solomon his son. ² "I am about to go the way of all the earth," he said. "So be strong, act like a man, ³ and observe what the Lord your God requires: Walk in obedience to him, and keep his decrees and commands, his laws and regulations, as written in the Law of Moses. Do this so that you may prosper in all you do and wherever you go ⁴ and that the Lord may keep his promise to me: 'If your descendants watch how they live, and if they walk faithfully before me with all their heart and soul, you will never fail to have a successor on the throne of Israel.' ⁵ Now you yourself know what Joab son of Zeruiah did to me—what he did to the two commanders of Israel's armies, Abner son of Ner and Amasa son of Jether. He killed them, shedding their blood in peacetime as if in battle, and with that blood, he stained the belt around his waist and the sandals on his feet. ⁶ Deal with him according to your wisdom, but do not let his gray head go down to the grave in peace. ⁷ But show kindness to the sons of Barzillai of Gilead and let them be among those who eat at your table. They stood by me when I fled from your brother Absalom. ⁸ And remember, you have with you Shimei son of Gera, the Benjamite from Bahurim, who called down bitter curses on me the day I went to Mahanaim. When he came down to meet me at the Jordan, I swore to him by the Lord: 'I will not put you to death by the sword.' ⁹ But now, do not consider him innocent. You are a man of wisdom; you will know what to do to him. Bring his gray head down to the grave in blood. ¹⁰ Then David rested with his ancestors and was buried in the City of David.¹¹ He had reigned forty years over Israel—seven years in Hebron and thirty-three in Jerusalem. ¹² So Solomon sat on the throne of his father David, and his rule was firmly established."*

The Strong man

The first instruction for Solomon from his father was to be strong and act like a man. He is told that strength is one of the virtues he would need for success. I like you have seen a many men raised up only to fall because of a lack of strength. We will need strength to get to our destiny and strength to remain there. There will be all kinds of opposition to your throne or Kingdom. There will be people jealous of your station in life and they do what they can to destroy you. When I was in school it was a badge of honor to get good grades, but now the badge is awarded to those who are not applying themselves. Therefore, the young people with abilities stop moving forward to fit in. These young people somewhere in the past lost their courage and strength to obtain their goals just to fit in.

One must be so passionate about reaching their God-given purpose, that they allow nothing to hinder them. A perfect example of this would be Solomon's son, who was not taught the same lesson or chose not to follow the examples of his fathers. When Rehoboam Solomon's son reaches the throne, they face the crisis of change. The people felt the burden of too many taxes. They approached the throne for a solution. Rehoboam had his piers that were counselors and he had older men from his dad's regime. The older men told him he should listen to the voice of the people and lift the burden but he chose to fit in with the younger crowd and caused such an uproar that the Kingdom was split in half. We lose so much because of a lack of strength to make the right decision when peer pressure is present. Strength is definitely a prerequisite to leadership.

Joshua was given this same instruction when his leader died and he took the reins. *Joshua 1: 1 "After the death of Moses the servant of the* L*ord, the* L*ord said to Joshua son of Nun, Moses' aide:* ² *Moses my servant is dead. Now then, you and all these people, get ready to cross the Jordan River into the land I am about to give to them—to the Israelites.* ³ *I will give you every place where you* set your foot, as I promised Moses. ⁴ *Your territory will extend from the desert to Lebanon, and from the great river, the Euphrates—all the Hittite country—to the Mediterranean Sea in the west.* ⁵ *No one will be able to stand against you all the days of your life. As I was with Moses, so I will be with you; I will never leave you nor forsake you.* ⁶ *Be strong and courageous, because you will lead these people to inherit the land I swore to their ancestors to give them.* ⁷ *"Be strong and very courageous. Be careful to obey all the law my servant Moses gave you; do not turn from it to the right or to the left, that you may be successful wherever you go."*

    Joshua had the daunting task of taking the same rebellious people into their inheritance. Sounds like pastoring, doesn't it? The common denominator in these cases was a King or general strength was needed. The enemy of your soul will do all he can to cause you to fail.

    The enemy tries to study the patterns of God to impede your growth. When God gives us direction, he very rarely tells you about all the opposition, you will face. He tells us you are the head and not the tail above only and not beneath and that no weapon formed against you shall prosper. However, let us face it some of us would not have obey God had he told us beforehand some of the things we have now faced. What is most important to God is the giving and the completion of a task and remaining with him so he will accomplish it through you. I am now reading a book that is transforming my life, while writing this book. One of the illustrations the author uses is of some infamous events that happen in our country, the U.S.A. It was the bombing of the World Trade Center in New York City on 9/11/2001. This event is still affecting our world. Nineteen men in the name of their god destroyed property and lives. We know that this was a terrible event but one must say that the perpetrators had strength or some may say a weakness that the mission was more important than their lives. It took strength. If we are to reach this generation it will take strength to stand up against the enemy who will do all he can to keep these people in the blindness and darkness he has surrounded them in. Kings need strength to make decisions that are not popular at their conception but you see the future results.

Teach your disciples by example to be strong. I remember the testimony of a minister who reached a gang leader for Christ in New York. The gangster pulled out a switchblade, and said to the minister that he would cut him into pieces. And the preacher responded that he would love him with every piece; now that took strength. Let us lean on the Lord for his strength to overcome the opposition we face in our journey. The strength of the believer is the Holy Spirit. The Holy Spirit is one person you cannot do without.

Listen to Paul's teaching to Ephesians 6: *[10] Finally, be strong in the Lord and in his mighty power. [11] Put on the full armor of God, so that you can take your stand against the devil's schemes. [12] For our struggle is not against flesh and blood, but against the rulers, against the authorities, against the powers of this dark world and against the spiritual forces of evil in the heavenly realms. [13] Therefore put on the full armor of God, so that when the day of evil comes, you may be able to stand your ground, and after you have done everything, to stand. [14] Stand firm then, with the belt of truth buckled around your waist, with the breastplate of righteousness in place, [15] and with your feet fitted with the readiness that comes from the gospel of peace. [16] In addition to all this, take up the shield of faith, with which you can extinguish all the flaming arrows of the evil one. [17] Take the helmet of salvation and the sword of the spirit, which is the word of God. [18] And pray in the spirit on all occasions with all kinds of prayers and requests. With this in mind, be alert and always keep on praying for all of the Lord's people. [19] Pray also for me, that whenever I speak, words may be given to me so that I will fearlessly make known the mystery of the gospel, [20] for which I am an ambassador in chains. Pray that I may declare it fearlessly, as I should."*

Our strength is in the Lord and the power of his might. If you try to rule in this earth with your strength, you are destined to fail. We are told to put on the amour of God. Satan is always trying to dethrone you and have you operate as a mere man. I will come back to this passage but to drive home my point let us look at Peter's teaching.

2Peter 1:3 *"His divine power has given us everything we need for a godly life through our knowledge of him who called us by his own glory and goodness. ⁴ Through these he has given us his very great and precious promises, so that through them you may participate in the divine nature, having escaped the corruption in the world caused by evil desires.*

     Peter tells us we have the ability to operate above human existence. The more knowledge of God you possess the more like him you become. We can participate in his Divine nature. Paul teaches us that everyone has a day of evil. I have had many days of evil attacks, and I am sure you have as well. Strength is needed to overcome in those days. Sickness is a day of evil, poverty is a day of evil, divorce is a day of evil, losing your job is a day of evil, conflict is a day of evil, you get the picture evil is always near. He tells us that the Gospel brings peace! With the devil's scheme, we will need God's peace. He instructs us that our enemy is spirit beings and not in the flesh so I must combat him with the weapons of the spirit and not of the flesh. What are these weapons? Truth is that which pertains to God. Righteousness= the condition acceptable to God. The Bible says that Abraham believed God and it was counted to him for righteousness. By putting your continual trust in God you are putting on righteousness. Feet prepared= we make our warfare with the Gospel and there with populate the Kingdom. The shield = our faith to protect you from the enemy's arrows. Helmet = salvation protects your thought life and gives you direction. Sword= is the word of God. This is how we fight off our enemy. We are not a part of a democracy but a Kingdom theocracy; God speaks and we respond. This sword is powerful in keeping your strength up. Because we have a Kingdom, we are not control by our ideas. When I am asked what my views on homosexuality are or abortion; I always respond by saying, I have no views but I will tell you what my King says. I say I am just the newspaper boy not the Editor. If you have a problem with this statement, take it up with the Editor (God). We must take them to the Word of God not your words.

We were told to pray in the spirit and to pray for all believers especially those in leadership. The one thing I keep going back to what Jesus said concerning God's house. He said it would be a house of prayer. Look at what he did not say, it is a house of preaching, or fellowship. These things are most important. But in order for you to remain strong, the word preached and the fellowship should lead you to ask God in prayer to meet your needs – and he will!

Look at what the writer of Hebrews says;

Hebrews 11:6 *"And without faith it is impossible to please God, because anyone who comes to him must believe that he exists and that he rewards those who earnestly seek him.*

First, we are in need of faith in God's existence, and secondly with that faith we need to come seeking him, and finally we need to know he will reward those who diligently seek him. If you would be honest, you do not serve God for nothing but you know there are benefits in serving him. One of my favorite stories in the Bible is that of David verse Goliath. Beyond common belief, David did not fight Goliath for nothing. If you look carefully at the story, you will find David asking one question at least three times to different individuals. What was his question? What will the man get for fighting this giant? The answer that he received was that his family would be tax- free, he would be enriched by the king and given the king's daughter in marriage. Now with the help of God and the motivation of reward he did go to battle. Preaching brings to me the faith I need to believe God. Fellowship puts me around others he has blessed and through prayer I am able to experience his reward. Teach your mentee like David when he fought Goliath, that there is reward time to every battle and reward is the great motivator. So notice not only God's presence and God's power but also is provision and reward that brings us great.

Act like a man

He was told to act like a man. Man was given authority on this earth. Genesis 1:*26 Then God said, "Let us make mankind in our image, in our likeness, so that they may rule over the fish in the sea and the birds in the sky, over the livestock and all the wild animals, [a] and over all the creatures that move along the ground." 27 So God created humankind in his own image, in the image of God he created them; male and female he created them. 28 God blessed them and said to them, "Be fruitful and increase in number; fill the earth and subdue it. Rule over the fish in the sea and the birds in the sky and over every living creature that moves on the ground.*

The reason God said he made man in his image is that like God he can rule on the earth. Man being made in the image of God he like God would have a sphere of influence. God is also a God of increase he made us where we too would expand. There is a parable in the New Testament where a master gives out talents or money and leaves with the expectation that on his return there would be a return on his money. When he returned two of the men invested the money and one buried it. The one that buried the money lost even that which he had. We are to be productive on the earth. God says a good man leaves and inheritance to his children and grandchildren. Life is not to be lived selfishly. God gives gifts and talents to produce on this earth for you and yours and the advancement of his Kingdom.

Chapter Three
The Kingdom Operates Under Covenant

David gave his son some very important task to carry out. He wanted him to know and to remember the origin of his Kingdom. He left him with these instructions found in the book of 1 Kings 2: *[3] "and observe what the LORD your God requires: Walk in obedience to him, and keep his decrees and commands, his laws and regulations, as written in the Law of Moses. Do this so that you may prosper in all you do and wherever you go."* He left him a pattern of sure success. Number one he was told to give close observation to the requirements of the Lord. David told his son not to be careless and forget that he too was under authority. When you read the books of the Kings, you find that many did forget and brought the country to great loss. David had a clear understanding of what he was instructing his son. First observation is to not lose sight. He did not want his son to turn his attention to something he thought more important and lose sight on God's word. Solomon did remember the teaching of his father, look what he said as he was issuing out his wisdom.

Proverbs 25: "These are more proverbs of Solomon, compiled by the men of Hezekiah king of Judah: [2] It is the Glory of God to conceal a matter; to search out a matter is the glory of kings. [3] As the heavens are high and the earth is deep, so the hearts of kings are unsearchable. [4] Remove the dross from the silver, and a silversmith can produce a vessel; [5] remove wicked officials from the king's presence, and his throne will be established through righteousness. [6] Do not exalt yourself in the king's presence, and do not claim a place among his great men; [7] it is better for him to say to you, "Come up here, than for him to humiliate you before his nobles."

What you have seen with your eyes:
Observation is important because there are things that

have not been revealed to the King. This is important, is the Glory of God to conceal a thing but the glory of the King to search it out. God said in another scripture "my ways are above yours" so if I am to know his ways I must keep up with him. He tells us in another "behold I do a new thing." Every person and every King must find what God is doing now. Coming through the wilderness the Israelites had to keep their focus on God, he was fire by night and a cloud by day. If God was to move and they not be aware of it they would suffer, the consequence of his absence. It is the same with you and I we must stay focus on God's movements. Many people are working for the Lord but not with him. Samson was a man of great strength and power. Yet he was brought to frailness because of losing sight of God. Arising to do only what was normal to him to find himself without God's presence when he needed him.

    David also instructed him to keep God's decrees, the dictionary defines "decree as an official order issued by a legal authority." If we are to take orders, we must first know that the one issuing the order is a legal authority. I did not serve in the arm forces but I have a great deal of respect for those who did. Nevertheless, of late, I have researched the different ranks from private to General and also the medals and badges of rank. Another soldier does not have to know the officer personally to obey him he just has to recognize his rank. Once rank is established he must honor, respect and obey the decrees issue by them, with the knowledge of some kind of penalty if he or she does not. David is telling his son Solomon you must respect God's rank and authority in the Kingdom.

    He was told to obey God's commands. Commands are described as telling someone to do something in a forceful an official way. Again, rank determines one's ability to give commands. Notice these are commands not suggestions. How does God give commands? The answer is through his words and through his servants? So why do we fight either when we know they have a legal right to do so. How many times have you heard God say to one of the leaders in the Bible to command the people to do something? So if his servants of the past had the ability to give commands, don't you think they would today? God said I am the same and he never changes. Therefore, if he did it yesterday he is still doing it today.

His laws and regulation were to be obeyed. Laws are a system of rules and guidelines and regulations. God has checks and balances in his system to make sure we carry out his wishes. Does obedience have no merit? This is the reason behind obedience that favors us we will be rewarded. David told Solomon that he would prosper in all that he did or where ever he would go by just taking these instructions. I found that as a soldier obeys and fulfills the requirements he is advanced in rank. Rank also brings honor and more privilege and reward. David tells his son that this also takes place in the Kingdom of God obedience and fulfillment of duty brings honor and rank. We must instruct this new generation of Kings that there is not away around obedience. Kings are in authority but also under authority.

David was promised that his Kingdom would be an everlasting Kingdom based on his obedience to God and His Word. This is a very important part of these verses listen to David. "Do this so that you may prosper in all you do and wherever you go" Prosperity on the earth is tied to obeying the rules of the Landlord. We are Kings but again he is The King and the one who inaugurated us. Psalm 24 plainly states. "The earth is the LORD's, and everything in it, the world, and all who live in it;" So our Kingdom was given to us with boundaries and requirements.

The last part of these instructions held the benefits. You will prosper wherever you go. It is most important that I reiterate that value of obedience. Success where ever you go. Listen to that success wherever you go. While sometimes we think, we are stupid for the decision to be a king with limited powers. We know that it comes with unlimited powers and authority. Obedience is not a sign of weakness but intelligent power. Faith is not working off ignorance but knowledge. Let us look at some things we know from the book of 1 John *"³ We know that we have come to know him if we keep his commands.⁴ Whoever says, "I know him," but does not do what he commands is a liar, and the truth is not in that person. ⁵ But if anyone obeys his word, love for God[a] is truly made complete in them. This is how we know we are in him:⁶ Whoever claims to live in him must live as Jesus did"*. We can only say we know him when we obey him. Kings who obey The King operate with great knowledge of The King. Disobedience is a sign you are a liar. It is very important to know God before trying to reign in his Kingdom. I was amazed to discover Jesus while on earth only cursed one thing. He rebuked many things but only cursed one. Hypocrisy! The fig tree in the gospels proclaimed to be something it was not and he cursed it. The word Hypocrite is where we get our word for actor. Therefore, obedience is a sign you know him and not pretentious. When we obey him according to this passage, he completes his love in us. Love is how you know you are operating in him. Therefore, Faith and obedience is not ignorance.

    I want you to notice what obedience would do. First it caused him to complete love in us thereby we know we are in him. Then it goes further, *"¹¹ But anyone who hates a brother or sister is in the darkness and walks around in the darkness. They do not know where they are going, because the darkness has blinded them."* Obedience is a sign you know where you are going. Love is a road sign that you are going in the right direction. Kings must know what time or season it is. The Bible tells us David understood this for he reached his generation and then he died. I am writing of this book, because I know what time it is. God wants me to share what he has placed in me that the next generations of Kings will have strength and a strong foundation to stand on. Listen to the cry of the Apostle's heart in these next verses on the subject of time. *"¹⁸ Dear children, this is the last hour; and as you have heard that the anti-Christ is coming, even now many antichrists have come. This is* *how we know it is the last hour. ^{19} They went out from us, but they did not really belong to us. For if they had belonged to us, they would have remained with us; but their going showed that none of them belonged to us."* Those of us who are in obedience to the King can tell the season by the obedience or lack of it. An anti-Christ movement will establish the last days. We will know that it is time to be serious about reaching this next generation when we see people against Christ and leaving the fold (the church). We need to be about our father's business because the time is at hand. Without obedience, we cannot even tell time. We that are obedient are not ignorant to Satan's devices. GOD again instruct us in his word concerning our knowledge. *"^{20} But you have an anointing from the Holy One, and all of you know the truth.* [e] *^{21} I do not write to you because you do not know the truth, but because you do know it and because no lie comes from the truth. ^{22} Who is the liar? It is whoever denies that Jesus is the Christ. Such a person is the anti-Christ—denying the Father and the Son. ^{23} No one who denies the Son has the Father; whoever acknowledges the Son has the Father also."*

John starts this off by saying that you know the truth. The truth is not just a group of foundational statements but also a person Jesus Christ and you know him. This knowledge of him raises your kingship to another level because if you know him you know the father. Because of our obedience, we know that anyone who denies the son has already denied the father.

Again, faith and obedience is not ignorance. We also know that you are not regal just because you are a man. The devil has been so deceiving by convincing us that we are the special one because we were born in a certain state in life. We have money and believe it or not some because they do not. Some people believe they are more spiritual because they do not have money. We believe our race is the chosen over everyone else on the earth. This is not limited to black or white you find this in nations where the people are the same race but you were not born in my tribe or your skin is darker than mine is. I had some oriental people in my church while I was pastoring in

Los Angeles, and they were from a part of the East. Their skin was darker than the others Orientals so they were considered inferior. The most segregated place on the planet is church on Sunday morning. Listen to the Apostle here "[29] If you know that he is righteous, you know that everyone who does what is right has been born of him." You must be born in the royal family and have knowledge that God is righteous, and that your obedience is a sign that you have been born in this family.

The thing that keeps us going, when here is opposition to our ministry, is the knowledge of who he is and who we are in him. Your Kingdom is in this world yet not a part of the chaos of this world. John warns us with something else he tells us we know. "See what great love the Father has lavished on us, that we should be called children of God!' That is who we are! The reason the world does not know us is that it did not know him. *[2] Dear friends, now we are children of God, and what we will be has not yet been made known. But we know that when Christ appears, [a] we shall be like him, for we shall see him as he is.[3] All who have this hope in him purify themselves, just as he is pure.*" We sometimes struggle for years with this, because we all have the desire to be loved, accepted and understood by the people of this world. You are so much like the King you serve that the world cannot tell you a part from him and this is the way it should be.

Someone shared this true story with me concerning a missionary that was being guided an indigenous African boy. When seeing another boy running through the jungle the boy threw the missionary to the ground and he prostrated himself as well. The missionary had never received this kind of treatment from the boy so he was overly concern. So, young boy began to explain his action to the missionary. He ask the missionary did he see the other boy running through the jungle and the missionary said he had, but did you notice he was carrying something yes said the missionary. The boy then explains that the boy was carrying the King's staff, which must be recognized and honored no matter whose hands it is in. Like this story, yes, we have problems because of our identification with the King but we also have authority because of it. Faith and obedience are keys to living as God planned. Obedience is a sign that our sins have been forgiven us, John again says *"⁴ Everyone who sins breaks the law; in fact, sin is lawlessness. ⁵ But you know that he appeared so that he might take away our sins. And in him is no sin. ⁶ No one who lives in him keeps on sinning. No one who continues to sin has either seen him or known him."*

Walking in disobedience is lawlessness, which is sin. Our sins are forgiven, so we do not continue to do what we have been forgiven for. We are certainly knowledgeable that God is dealing with our sins and grateful that he is. We thank him, praise him and sometimes are overwhelmed with emotions because of it. We are very grieved when we fail God. We are faithful and obedient out of knowledge of reward and not ignorance. We are knowledgeable of our family members by their obedience to the King. John again explains *"⁹ No one who is born of God will continue to sin, because God's seed remains in them; they cannot go on sinning, because they have been born of God. ¹⁰ This is how we know who the children of God are and who the children of the devil are: Anyone who does not do what is right is not God's child, nor is anyone who does not love their brother and sister."* God's seed in you helps you to remain faithful to Him. He places first his Spirit in you. This means the very presence of God along with his eternal word is on the inside of you. Remember David is teaching his son to be King. David made the statement "thy word have I hid in my heart so I might not sin against thee." The seed in us protects us from disobeying the King.

We know that the length of our reign is grounded in our obedience. The book of John overflows with the truth of what we know: *"¹¹ For this is the message you heard from the beginning: We should love one another. ¹² Do not be like Cain, who belonged to the evil one and murdered his brother. Moreover, why did he murder him? Because his own actions were, evil and his brothers were righteous. ¹³ Do not be surprised, my brothers and sisters,* [b] *if the world hates* you. ¹⁴ We know that we have passed from death to life, because we love each other. Anyone who does not love remains in death. ¹⁵ Anyone who hates a brother or sister is a murderer, and you know that no murderer has eternal life residing in him." Our obedience lets us know when our rein begins and how long it will last. David is telling his son that obedience increases his reign. So again, faith and obedience are knowledge based.

Our obedience dictates our action. John speaks *"¹⁶ This is how we know what love is: Jesus Christ laid down his life for us. And we ought to lay down our lives for our brothers and sisters. ¹⁷ If anyone has material possessions and sees a brother or sister in need but has no pity on them, how can the love of God be in that person? ¹⁸ Dear children, let us not love with words or speech but with actions and in truth."*

If you are truly, obeying God the world will be a better place because you live. When God rewards you, he does it not just for you but that you can be a blessing. Remember what you teach must be something you live. When David became King, one of his first official operations was the very thing John is teaching. He summons his advisors and asks this question: "Is there anyone left in the household of Saul so I can bless him for Jonathan his father sakes?" I think it is noteworthy that the person he blessed had nothing to offer him back. Many times, we give to people and we expect to get back from them. The man that David blessed was a cripple and lived in the ghetto of that day. Listen to what God told Abraham in Genesis 12: *The LORD had said to Abram, "Go from your country, your people and your father's household to the land I will show you. ² "I will make you into a great nation, and I will bless you; I will make your name great, and you will be a blessing.* [a] *³ I will bless those who bless you, and whoever curses you I will curse; and all peoples on earth will be blessed through you."* [b]

There would be great reward for his obedience to God. He would make him a great nation, give him a great name, make him a blessing and every nation would be blessed because of him. I traveled a lot with a great man of

God. He was a modern day Apostle Paul yes like all men had failures and shortcomings but he was the closest I have seen to a modern day apostle. His name was Archbishop Benson Andrew Idahosa. Our team sometimes would be large he would introduce pastors, prophets, apostles, evangelist, teachers and when it was my time he would say and this is a king. I would be so embarrassed because I did not feel like a King and would rather he not introduce that way. I remember being on the plane to return to the states from Nigeria. He left the plane then came back on just to say to me you are a king act like it. I finally got over my embarrassment and accepted what he was trying to develop in me.

I have since helped others with this struggle. I was in the country of Surinam, in South America, we had a great healing ministry there and God did great wonders like opening up blind eyes and many other notable miracles. I am so embarrassed to say I do not remember this wonderful woman's name but she was a great woman of God and was the wife of the president of that nation. She asks my host to bring me to her office to meet with her and they did. I was delighted to meet her but I was wondering what the nature of my visit was. When I met her, she was a delightful God-fearing woman who loved her King Jesus. This nation is filled with many religions Hinduism, Islam, along with many others she was a Christian working alongside these people every day and feeling the oppression that it brought. She wanted me to council with her and pray for her and therefore I did.

However, there was one more great concern that this mighty woman had she was very soft spoken and humble. Remember she is the president's wife and the people of her nation honor her in this position. This was her concern because to her it was taking something from Jesus for them to honor her in this way. God had me to explain to her that Jesus is the King of Kings, so how can Jesus be King of Kings if there are not any other Kings. She was so relieved that she was not doing anything wrong while she was being honored as a king.

If you noticed in this passage to Abraham that God is not intimidated by man's achievements he makes them great and gives them a great name. If you look, at Abraham, his name was once Abram but God added a part of his own name to it to create Abraham and the same with Sarah. We see again that Faith and Obedience is not a sign of ignorance but knowledge of reward. David himself understood this principle when he fought Goliath, there was reward tied to fighting the giant. He asked three times, what will the man get that fights this giant? He was told he would be enriched, his family would pay no taxes and he would marry the Kings daughter. This was the will of God for David and his chance to get close enough to the King for training. So many people want to reign like someone they know but will not submit himself or herself to no one for training. This is something I learned early if you want to be blessed learn from someone who is.

There is an acronym I read F.A.T, one must be Faithful, Available and Teachable. Without these virtues, no one can help you reach your goal. If we could just understand this one thing, there are no self-made men all of us learn from one another. Remember all knowledge comes from God and he passed it on to men and they pass it on to others. I have been blessed to have my youngest grandchild living with us. Her name is Cali, God has allowed me to see this principle at work in her life: first to crawl, now she is walking and we are helping her form some words. Her training has already begun. Like a sponge she is soaking it all in. Now for her to operate on this earth she has to put her trust in the other humans that she is surrounded by. You too are a product of your environment. Look at the people that you are around and you are looking at your future. My mother used to tell me birds of a feather flock together. You will never be a king hanging with jester. Jesters will help you become a Jester. You need a David in your life to become King.

There is a well-known business writer in one of his books he mention something concerning this. He said that "he has many friends and acquaintances who often ask him for two things. One they will ask for a loan or they will ask for a job. Very few ask him what does it take to reach your success." If you desire to be a king you need information, the first of this should come from the King of Kings, which you can discover in his manual called the Bible. Then you should search out a king who has discovered the King of Kings methods and learn from them. You can learn from their successes and failures. I am very careful with a book that I am reading when I gain insight on some subject that is of great interest to me. I guard it and protect it from injury because to me it is the lifeblood of the writer's mind and heart. I feel they are there speaking to me and giving me instructions. I think I mentioned before the love and respect I have for the men and women in my life that helped shape me. I saw something while traveling in Nigeria that is missing in our country. The Nigerians respect those who have helped them accomplish great things in their life, they bow in respect to their teachers and their pastors. We sometimes take for granted what others add to our lives. If you really understood, what it takes to prepare a lesson for school or a sermon for Sunday you would be more appreciative of your leaders. People could get theirs and tell you to get yours.

    There are people who would sacrifice much for you to reach your goal. David as he is training Solomon must have reflected on at least two people who helped him to reach his goal. He would have never been there without the help of the Lord. However, there were others who helped him first there was the Prophet Samuel who anointed him. You must understand that the person who licensed or ordained you was on a mission from God to anoint the chosen one. This person would have to go beyond his own prejudices to see that you were the one. Like David, you probably did not fit the mold of which the prophet thought God could use. He or she had to listen to hear the voice of God clearly. You only looked like someone who should be on the back of the desert-tending sheep. Surrendering their pursuit of you was not an option until you were in the place where God wanted you to be. I was at the altar in the first church God allowed me to start. I was praying at the altar there were others at that same altar when I looked to my right and saw a young man who had just given his life to the Lord. As I gazed upon him, the Spirit of the Lord spoke to me and said that is your new youth pastor. I remember arguing with God reminding God this boy came out of a traditional church and he did not know anything about being a youth pastor. God said, yes I know you will train him. I obeyed God instructions, God was right that boy became a great youth pastor and even greater pastor. He pastors in the same city that I trained him in. His name is Pastor Luther Whitfield and even to this day, I am glad I obeyed God. Alongside of him we trained another man, his name was John Ramsey and he pastors a great church in Indianapolis, Indiana. We are not as close as I would like us to be but, it is ok they are still in the service of the King I did what was the right thing to do.

There was another person in the life of David that helped him to reach is goal. This man was Jonathan; remember he was Saul's son and heir apparent to the throne. Jonathan's life changed and so did his destiny when he met David. The Bible says that their love went beyond that of women. He saw something in David that he did not have in his own life and was willing to step back so that David could shine. Jonathan was nothing like his father Saul. Saul was haughty, prideful, and fearful and intimidated by the destiny of another. He recognized that God had destined David for the throne even though it was his birthright to be King. He told David that he would be second in the Kingdom and David would be number one. They actually made a blood covenant with each other and Jonathan removed his robe and gave it to David. This man saw the will of God as something greater than his own will. There are still some Jonathans around who would be willing to give up their career for the advancement of yours if they sense the presence of God in your life, and your will to obey God. All we need to do is to stay in the will of

God and help from God will come. Sounds like a Biblical principle to me. "Seek you first the Kingdom of God and his righteous and all these things shall be added unto you."

Chapter Four
Walking in Agreement with the King

David continued in his training of the new king with some startling advice.

1 Kings 2: *⁵ "Now you yourself know what Joab son of Zeruiah did to me—what he did to the two commanders of Israel's armies, Abner son of Ner and Amasa son of Jether. He killed them, shedding their blood in peacetime as if in battle, and with that blood, he stained the belt around his waist and the sandals on his feet. ⁶ Deal with him according to your wisdom, but do not let his gray head go down to the grave in peace.⁷ "But show kindness to the sons of Barzillai of Gilead and let them be among those who eat at your table. They stood by me when I fled from your brother Absalom.⁸ "And remember, you have with you Shimei son of Gera, the Benjamite from Bahurim, who called down bitter curses on me the day I went to Mahanaim. When he came down to meet me at the Jordan, I swore to him by the* LORD: *'I will not put you to death by the sword.' ⁹ But now, do not consider him innocent. You are a man of wisdom; you will know what to do to him. Bring his gray head down to the grave in blood."*

I have seen so many ministers pushed in a corner by reporters trying to embarrass them and to make them look narrow minded before the public. These things happen for a reason so that their agenda could be pushed down the throats of the public without the church blocking it. The church and the pastors must made to look ignorant in order to fulfill their agenda. Sadly enough we sometimes fall prey to the enemies tactics. One way to avoid this is to separate you from what the King said. We take too many things personally and we get deeply hurt by a challenge to God's word. I found that God is strong enough to handle any opposition to what he said. Notice in this passage David is reminding the new king of some past attacks on the Kingdom as well as some people that had been a great help. He is told to deal with David's enemy using the instructions David is giving him. So these were

David's enemy. David's enemies automatically became his. I want you to stay with me on this. You did not have a problem with Satan until you became a Christian. The moment you became a Christian, God's enemy became your enemy. So not knowing anything about this enemy, you had to fight with the knowledge given you from the original enemy of your enemy (God). God taught us how to fight this enemy.

Let us look at a few of his instructions. Ephesians 6: *[10]" Finally, be strong in the Lord and in his mighty power. [11] Put on the full armor of God, so that you can take your stand against the devil's schemes. [12] For our struggle is not against flesh and blood, but against the rulers, against the authorities, against the powers of this dark world and against the spiritual forces of evil in the heavenly realms. [13] Therefore put on the full armor of God, so that when the day of evil comes, you may be able to stand your ground, and after you have done everything, to stand. [14] Stand firm then, with the belt of truth buckled around your waist, with the breastplate of righteousness in place, [15] and with your feet fitted with the readiness that comes from the gospel of peace. [16] In addition to all this, take up the shield of faith, with which you can extinguish all the flaming arrows of the evil one. [17] Take the helmet of salvation and the sword of the spirit, which is the word of God. [18] And pray in the spirit on all occasions with all kinds of prayers and requests. With this in mind, be alert and always keep on praying for all the Lord's people. [19] Pray also for me, that whenever I speak, words may be given me so that I will fearlessly make known the mystery of the gospel, [20] for which I am an ambassador in chains. Pray that I may declare it fearlessly, as I should."* 1 Peter 5: [8] *"Be alert and of sober mind. Your enemy the devil prowls around like a roaring lion looking for someone to devour. [9] Resist him, standing firm in the faith, because you know that the family of believers throughout the world is undergoing the same kind of sufferings."*

2 Corinthians 10: [3]*" For though we walk in the flesh, we do not war after the flesh: [4] (For the weapons of our warfare are not carnal, but mighty through God to the pulling down of strong holds;) [5] Casting down imaginations, and every high thing that exalteth itself against the knowledge of God, and bringing into captivity every thought to the obedience of Christ; [6] And having in a readiness to revenge all disobedience, when your obedience is fulfilled".*

In order for us to deal with God's enemy we must take heed to God's instructions because we do not know his tactics.

God's enemies are now mine and I must follow instructions while dealing with them. So when people ask me what is my opinion about abortion or homosexuality for example? I tell them I have no opinions but a word from the King. I will also remind them that the King's enemies are now mine. If you are a part of the Kingdom, his enemies are yours as well, so where do you stand? Moving from there David also reminded Solomon of some people who had served him well and was due to be treated as such. The Bible tells us to do good to all men but especially to the household of faith. To those who have served him well. One of the least attended services in some churches should be one of the most attended. That is the celebration of the pastor. The Bible tells us the he or she is worth double honor. It is amazing that God allows some of us to live, the way we treat his servant. David on his deathbed is still thinking on the good deeds that others had done for him. God said I will not forget your labor of love. Men may forget but God will not. What God hates and yes he does hate we should hate, and what God loves we should love. You should have a love for the servants of the Lord. I have some children I love very much, some biological and other who come to me and I love all of them. What if someone would approach me for assistance and I was in a position to honor their request; However, they preface it by saying I do not like your children, I would do whatever I could to hurt them but please give me what I need. That seems laughable and very prideful for someone to approach you or me like that, yet we approach God like that all the time. We cannot stand one of his children but we want his help in our situations.

    We are some bold people aren't we? You must realize that you are a citizen of a Kingdom. A Kingdom is the domain of a King. A Kingdom is not a democracy where you make choices on what you like or dislike. When you were born into the Kingdom, you made your choice to like what the King likes and to dislike what he does not. You do not choose conservatism or a liberal view it is only the King's view. We want to divide God's word up into our views. We have the social gospel, the evangelical, the word of faith, I believe the King espouses all those views at one time or another we cannot hold only to the one that fits our agenda. He is the King we are the citizens. He speaks we respond.

Chapter Five
Steps to Kingdom Success

There are principles to getting anywhere you want to go and that include working and operating in the Kingdom of God. In training your new king they must adapt to the Kingdom views.

Step 1 - Sanctify your desires:

Put your ambition on the back burner so you can fulfill the desires of the King. The sanctification of your desires is so important, why you might ask? Let us again ask Mark. Mark 11: [24] *"Therefore I say unto you, what things so ever ye desire, when ye pray, believe that ye receive them, and ye shall have them"*.

My desires are linked to what the King will do for me. As a child of God it places you in the royal family, it comes with privileges. One of those privileges is that God will give us the desires of our heart. I am not referring to the physical heart, but I am talking about our inner man or human spirit. The heart of a man is the engine that runs the man. The heart has form, shape and abilities. We know that the heart has the ability to think. The Bible says, "As a man thinks in his heart so is he". The heart according to scripture can become bitter. We know that before surrendering to Christ that our heart is dead to the things of Christ and rebellious. When we come to Christ, a process is begun to sanctify the heart or set it apart for Christ and the things of God. A friend from South Africa told me, when you mine for gold, there is a process of removing the gold that is quick when you use machines. The most difficult thing about this process was removing the mountain from the gold. It is the same with us and God; on a particular day, God snatches us from darkness into his marvelous light, from death to life. Then the real task of removing the world from us began. We have had many years operating in the world as a son of God's enemy Satan. While we were his enemy, guess what was some of his requirements. To love what he loves and to hate what he hates. Does that sound familiar? Yes, our King requires the same thing. Remember he warned us we could not serve two masters this is why you will either love the one or hate the other. God in 1 John shares this with us. 1 John 2: [15]*"Love not the world, neither the things that are in the world. If any man love the world, the love of the Father is not in him.* [16]*For all that is in the world, the lust of the flesh, and the lust of the eyes, and the pride of life, is not of the Father, but is of the world.* [17]*And the world passeth away, and the lust thereof: but he that doeth the will of God abideth forever."*

He tells us to watch where we put our devotion. We for years have used our senses to operate in and to create our world. We now have to be trained to use the faith that comes from our heart. We all understand the lust of the flesh. Which one of us has not lusted for something in our lifetime? We know that our eyes have seen things and lust for it. We all have dealt with the spirit of pride. We want everyone to know who we are. Is God telling us now that we will never have these kind of temptations? No. I have shared on many occasion the temptations that I have been through. The more we yield our spirit to Christ the more these things and the love for them began to fade. When we find out that the power over these temptations is found in the word of God. 1 John 2: [3]*"And hereby we do know that we know him, if we keep his commandments.* [4]*He that saith, I know him, and keepeth not his commandments, is a liar, and the truth is not in him.* [5]*But whoso keepeth his word, in him verily is the love of God perfected: hereby know we that we are in him.* [6]*He that saith he abideth in him ought himself also so to walk, even as he walked."*

Your walk becomes the same as Christ when we study and apply the word of God. Sanctification is to be set apart away from one thing and to another. God tells us in another place what he does for those who set themselves apart. Psalms 37: [3] *"Trust in the* L<small>ORD</small>, *and do good; so shalt thou dwell in the land, and verily thou shalt be fed.* [4]*Delight thyself also in the* L<small>ORD</small>: *and he shall give thee the desires of thine heart."*

You see, reading your Bible alone will not finish the sanctification process. However, when we obey his commands it is a sign that something on the inside has changed. Notice in this scripture, your heart has found something it delights in more than what the world offers. You must see the importance of this because the world has a lot to offer. I remember hearing someone give a testimony that when they were in the world they did not have any fun. Then someone else told them if you didn't have fun you were not doing it right. Moses testified he would rather suffer with the children of Israel than to enjoy the pleasures of sin for a season. The problem with sin is not its lack of pleasure but its expiration date. Both in Psalms 38 and 1 John 2, we were told that these pleasures along with this world have an expiration date. Every year I discovered even my ability to sin changed. Yet God remained the same, faithful. Whenever God tells you to sanctify he is about to give you an experience that you have never had.

Joshua 3: [5]*" And Joshua said unto the people, sanctify yourselves: For tomorrow, the* L<small>ORD</small> *will do wonders among you.* "Sanctification will not destroy you. First, it will move you from the temporary state and place you into something permanent, next, it will show you experiences that without it you will never know. In conclusion, God is willing to give you a blank check to write and cash it in his name if he can trust what is in your heart. Listen to these wonderful words? "Whatsoever things you desire when you pray believe you receive them and you shall have them." When your desires change and your appetite is now about advancing the Kingdom, God can trust your heart to ask for the right thing.

One last thing, sanctification brings about exaltation. 1 Peter 5: [6]*"Humble yourselves therefore under the mighty hand of God, that he may exalt you in due time:"* God's Kingdom is advanced when yours is. I do not want you to forget that he is the KING of KINGS. His Kingdom encompasses all of his king's kingdoms. So the more you advance the more his Kingdom does. There is no sanctification without humility. Humility has you to give up your way for another. Humility is not the absence of strength but the yielding of that strength to another. Who is the strongest the horse or the rider? Of course, the horse is but he places all of that strength under the control of another. That is what humility does. When you hear the word of the Lord and say that you understand it, if you understand it, then you stand under it. Humility is a virtue only wise Kings possess. Remember David is counseling is son King Solomon. Solomon was declared the wisest King, first he listened to his father then he submitted to the counsel of his father. Humility does not take away your Kingdom but adds to it. Philippians 2: *[3]" Let nothing be done through strife or vainglory; but in lowliness of mind let, each esteem others better than themselves. [4] Look not every man on his own things, but every man also on the things of others. [5] Let this mind be in you, which was also in Christ Jesus: [6] Who, being in the form of God, thought it not robbery to be equal with God: [7] But made himself of no reputation, and took upon him the form of a servant, and was made in the likeness of men: [8] And being found in fashion as a man, he humbled himself, and became obedient unto death, even the death of the cross. [9] Wherefore God also hath highly exalted him, and given him a name, which is above every name."*

    Glory is not glory unless it is achieved through Kingdom principles. Solomon in part of his life slipped away into the things of the world and finally recognized and taught on the subject of vanity. He said vanity is a like a vapor one minute is here and another it is gone. God promised us in this passage if you would humble yourself he would exalt you in due season. There are powerful truths in this passage I do not want you to miss and for years, I did. First, humility is a change of focus. The second thing is that humility is a mindset not and event. Just because you were humble at one time does not help you now. We must put on the mind of Christ. The only way this can happen is that you study his mind in the word, pray to continue in his mind and practice the use of his mind. Thirdly, you need to be comfortable in being you. Jesus knew who he was and did not think he was doing anything wrong because of this knowledge. The fourth component of humility is that it can't be forced on you. Jesus had to make himself of no reputation; no one else could do that. Humility does not erase who you are it magnifies it. Fifth, to place yourself, in a state lower than who you really are. Humility will cause you to endure what you would have ordinarily challenged. I went to Bible College in a community completely different from mine. I faced some things I would love to forget but they were placed in my life to change and help me become the leader I am today. Humility is a training ground. I am sure you know that in Bible College you are required to go to church. I love my church and my pastor but because I was new to them and they were new to me, you come in with preconceived ideas. An Elder would turn his face in the opposite direction so not to look me in the face when he served me communion. I was on a mission from God to learn his word nothing was going to run me away. I heard all the racial jokes possible.

When I started the church, we had a camp and my kids every year were given the worst of the sleeping conditions. Many of kids coming from their backgrounds did not even notice it, they were just glad to be there. I was a part of the presbytery and there were many committees formed for many occasions some of the men led two or three, I was never asked to lead any. When I asked why, I was told I needed to bring in more people like me so I could be a leader. When I left to start a new work, I was asked to preach at my church and a certain amount of money was raised to aid me in the mission. I received about a third of the money. I thank God that I know who I am. You see I had may opportunities to become bitter or resentful but I chose to humble myself for the task ahead. So our desires must be sanctified in order for us to operate in this new Kingdom.

Step 2: Your Faith must be placed in the God that fulfilled Desires

Mark 11: [22] "And Jesus answering saith unto them, Have faith in God. [23] For verily I say unto you, That whosoever shall say unto this mountain, Be thou removed, and be thou cast into the sea; and shall not doubt in his heart, but shall believe that those things which he saith shall come to pass; he shall have whatsoever he saith. [24] Therefore I say unto you, what things so ever ye desire, when ye pray, believe that ye receive them, and ye shall have them."

This step is most important for the advancement of your Kingdom and that of the Kingdom of God. Like Jesus, you must get your trainee as well as yourself to trust God. Faith will lead you places only God can bring you through. David in training his son, he knew how important this step was. David had been through all of the abuse of being the younger child and overlooked when it came to things that are deemed important. If you remember, David was not invited when the prophet Samuel came to visit. When they discovered it was David they had to go and find him. Only faith can carry you through times of rejection if not you will yield to bitterness. When David went to carry his brothers a meal and discovered they were afraid to face the giant David was ridiculed for his decision to face Goliath. Faith is needed to face these kinds of attacks from your own cowardly family. When facing the giant he was ridiculed because of his youth and size. To face the giants of life and everyone has them; you need to have the assurance that someone greater than you can bring you out. After defeating your giant, you now know all will now recognize that God is with you, only to face jealousy because he is. Saul want a soldier like David, but then deceived him and gave his wife to another. David understood the need of this principle of having faith in God. David also did things in his life to self-destruct. He took another man's wife and had that man killed. You must have faith to believe you will be forgiven when you repent.

This past evening I had the pleasure of having my cousins from Indiana in my home. My cousin Juanita brought a copy of a sermon preached by a very close friend of mine. The most of the sermon was the testimony of the preacher. He and I went to Bible College together; he was one of the people God used to get me to himself. He is a country boy with a heart of gold, but he had a weakness for women. He and a girl in our church began seeing one another. I knew this was not the will of God for him and told him so. To make a long story short I will say the relationship ended tragically. He being close enough to God to hear him broke the relationship off. She was not having it came and shot him he was able to get the gun and killed her. In his testimony, he states that the greatest thing he faced was dealing with the guilt and believing God could forgive. Through the faith, he learned earlier from his mother he was able to return to the God of mercy. I spoke with him lately and he is now working with people who faced some of the same things in their life. It was the principle of trusting God no matter what the situation is that brought him back from destroying himself because of guilt.

Faith in God will move your mountain. Faith is first conceived in the heart then expressed from the mouth and the God of desires moves your mountain. Notice God is going to give you your desires because you believe what he says. What a God we serve even the faith we need to believe him he gives to us as a gift. No greater words than this have been spoken. Ephesians 2: [4] "But God, who is rich in mercy, for his great love wherewith he loved us, [5] Even when we were dead in sins, hath quickened us together with Christ, (by grace ye are saved.) [6] And hath raised us up together, and made us sit together in heavenly places in Christ Jesus: [7] That in the ages to come he might shew the exceeding riches of his grace in his kindness toward us through Christ Jesus. [8] For by grace are ye saved through faith; and that not of yourselves: it is the gift of God". What a blessing, God found us dead and gave us his life. Afterwards he raised us up to a position to reign with him.

WOW! There was song back in the day a man was bragging about what he had done for his lady that fits what God actually did. "Didn't I blow your mind this time didn't I". Look all we need is our desires and the faith to receive them comes from the God of desires. Faith comes by hearing and hearing by the word of God. Why don't we try this we have tried everything else?

Step 3: General and specialized knowledge

General knowledge: 2 Peter 1: [3] *"According as his divine power hath given unto us all things that pertain unto life and godliness, through the knowledge of him that hath called us to glory and virtue:*

[4] *Whereby are given unto us exceeding great and precious promises: that by these ye might be partakers of the divine nature, having escaped the corruption that is in the world through lust".*

Specialized: Proverb 22: [6] *"Train up a child in the way he should go: and when he is old, he will not depart from it".* This is one of the most important principles. This is how we develop in the Kingdom. One of the ways we know we have a healthy child is to participate and watch their development. I know I have never mentioned this before in this book, but my beautiful granddaughter Cali and her parents are here with us at the writing of this book. Every step of her development had to be monitored by her parents Jonathan and Krystal or my wife and I. Her first words came from the knowledge she gain from one of us. When she crawled the first time we were there motivating her that she could do it. Oh, my God when she made her first steps we were all there camera in hand. I even took pictures of her at the piano at six months old. You know that everyone's grandchild is brilliant. Of course she can play, not. Nevertheless, there I was trying to teach her scales, chords and songs. I brought all this up because we need knowledge to go forward in Kingdom business. I have discovered that the problem is not in the learning as much as the will to learn and advance.

In our case as Kingdom builders, we need the expert help of a Kingdom builder. **Hebrews 12:2.** *"Looking unto Jesus the author and finisher of our faith; who for the joy that was set before him endured the cross, despising the shame, and is set down at the right hand of the throne of God".*

This scripture tells us to look to Jesus because he started us and will finish us. In the previous verses, Peter tells us that he has already given us everything we need for life and godliness. The finish life Peter explained God has given is hidden in the seed of his word or the knowledge of him. Therefore, as Kings we need to search the manuscripts of Jesus to discover this life. Proverbs 25:2 *"It is the Glory of God to conceal a thing: but the honor of kings is to search out a matter".* The fulfilled life is hidden in the knowledge of God and we need to search it out. The glories of your Kingdom and the virtues are discovered when you discover him. It is our weak nature or the nature of the natural man that gets in the way of our success. The solution is found and revealed by Peter that instructs us to get the knowledge of him which will subordinate your abase nature and allows you to put on his divine nature. This divine nature gives you the power and authority to live above natural man and his limitations. This is what I call general studies and every believer must take these courses. These are the require studies to operate in the Kingdom. Jesus said "when you see me you have seen the father." So my studies of Christ; also at the same time reveals the father. However, the Kingdom also has like any majoruniversity selective studies. First, everyone like in the universities needs the basic studies, or generalized studies. However, when you choose a career, you start taking studies in your field. The scripture, ([6]"Train up a child in the way he should go: and when he is old, he will not depart from it") deals with this. We have used this scripture to force something down the throat of our children; we have used it to discipline our children. This scripture while it might include or imply some of these things, it is to mostly point the child toward a specialize life style. Some parents have tried to live their failed lives out through their children. We try to turn children who loath sports in to athletes. Then turn great athletes into musicians or other parts of the arts.

In this passage, God is asking us to observe and point. He is not asking us to create, he asking us to observe what he has placed in the child and point them in that direction. Remember Peter said he has already given us what we need for life that is both general specific. All that is needed is discovery. Even when it comes to your children, this scripture is to be relied on. It is the Glory of God to conceal a thing but the wisdom of Kings discovers it. Kings relax and watch your child there will be some telltale event in their life that will show you what God placed there. If your child is an athlete, musician, painter, architect, missionary, politician or preacher it will be discovered. Let God be designer and you discoverer. What a team you and God can be.

Step 4: Program your spirit for success

Psalms 1:1 *Blessed is the man that walketh not in the counsel of the ungodly, nor standeth in the way of sinners, nor sitteth in the seat of the scornful. ² But his delight is in the law of the Lord; and in his law doth he meditate day and night. ³ And he shall be like a tree planted by the rivers of water, that bringeth forth his fruit in his season; his leaf also shall not wither; and whatsoever he doeth shall prosper".*

You must choose your counselors and mentors carefully. When you realize that, those whose input will guide your walk or your life style, you will choose wisely. This is where your spirit comes in. You have a human spirit that has been given life by the Holy Spirit and fed knowledge from the word of God, so God can lead and guide you by his spirit. When your spirit has been born again and you eat the word daily, you can know the voice of God even though you may not have heard or even experienced what is been said you can make a rightful judgment. I had come out of a traditional church that taught us against miracles.

As a young preacher when I was doing what I understood leading people to Christ. I was interrupted by a voice deep down inside of me showing me a woman who was twisted and needed assistance to even walk with a cane. The voice told me to tell the woman that he would heal her. I was terrified not because of the voice I knew the voice I had train my spirit to know the voice of God the devil and even my human flesh. This was the voice of God, but with information, I had yet to experience. But I knew this voice. I wrestled inside my soul which is me minded with my spirit which is God mined with this new information. Finally, I succumbed to the voice of God and responded. I told the woman that God said he would heal her. Thank God, I obeyed the voice of the Lord. But, then he speaks again and said tell her to throw those canes down. The fight with my soul and spirit was on again. Knowing who was speaking gave me relief but I felt challenged. I heard someone say God will never give you anything impossible to do but it will be irrational. This was not impossible it sure was irrational but obeying the voice I knew brought wonderful results. This woman dropped her canes and took off running around the church perfectly healed. I had never experience anything like this but the voice I knew. To operate as a king under a king you must know the voice of the King. Listen these verses will show how important this is. 1 Timothy **4** "Now the spirit speaketh expressly, that in the latter times some shall depart from the faith, giving heed to seducing spirits, and doctrines of devils; [2] speaking lies in hypocrisy; having their conscience seared with a hot iron;"

The Holy Spirit the administrator of the church warns us of coming danger. First, the demons have a doctrine. I wish time would permit me to tell you my whole story I was demon possessed before surrendering to Christ. I had powers that some of you would not believe. The other thing I had was a doctrine that was given to me straight from the spirit world. I was not aware of it when I was possessed I thought I had something from God. You must understand I was one of Satan's soldiers it was easy for him to deceive me but this passage says he will deceive believers. When I became a Christian and entered Bible College, some of our studies led us to the study of cults and the occults. I was amazed when we studied the New Age movement. I had never been a part of any organized group practicing the occult, but the doctrine they were explaining to me I already knew it, because it was given to me by the devil himself.

    The demons have a doctrine. So it is important that I can distinguish between demons and God. Both of them are in the spirit world. So you can be deceived. I saw the miraculous long before coming to Christ. Because a thing is spiritual does not mean the origin is God. Many people run to people who operate in the spirit world seeking help without knowing the origin of that help. God in this first division of Psalms tells us to watch where we get counsel. We are also warned that our fellowship with sinners will have a devastating effect on our spirit. We are not to be among the scorners either. Your mouth is a betrayal of your heart. Your mouth is the dispenser of your heart what comes out of your mouth is from your heart. Let us stay in prayer, praise, and fellowship with other believers, study the word of God and practice his presence so your Kingdom will be an extension of Jesus Kingdom.

Kingship Examination

- According to Psalms 8, You were made
    1. Just like the Angels
    2. Never to listen to anyone
    3. A little lower than the Angels (Elohim-God)
    4. All of the above

- You were made
    1. An animal
    2. An Angel
    3. Like God
    4. None of the above

- Being a King you are to
    1. Listen only to God
    2. Submit to another King for even more growth and authority
    3. To be in control at all times
    4. None of the above

- You can be born a King but still need be developed as a King
    1. True
    2. False

- David trained Solomon

1. True
2. False

- **Being a King Solomon was told to obey God's word**
    1. True
    2. False

- **Being a King he was told to act like a man (to walk in the authority given in Genesis 1:26)**
    1. True
    2. False

- **He was told to be the enemy of David's enemies**
    1. True
    2. False

- **He was told to love what David loves**
    1. True
    2. False

King to do list

- Do I respect the King that is mentoring me
- Is he following Christ then I should follow him or her
- I will learn to love what they love, God's word, God's people, God's work
- I will hate what they hate, the devil, sin, rebellious people
- I will follow their instructions

Chapter Six
God's Method was a Sign

Joshua 4: ⁴ So Joshua called together the twelve men he had appointed from the Israelites, one from each tribe, ⁵ and said to them, "Go over before the ark of the LORD your God into the middle of the Jordan. Each of you is to take up a stone on his shoulder, according to the number of the tribes of the Israelites, ⁶ to serve as a sign among you. In the future, when your children ask you, 'What do these stones mean?' ⁷ tell them that the flow of the Jordan was cut off before the ark of the covenant of the LORD. When it crossed the Jordan, the waters of the Jordan were cut off. These stones are to be a memorial to the people of Israel forever."

God not only sees us individually but he sees us collectively. The Lord only gave Joshua new instruction when the whole nation has crossed. A lot of us it is very different to see us the church as part of a Kingdom. Some because the country or environment we were raised in taught individuality. God makes statements like this if my people who are called by name would humble themselves and pray he would here from heaven and heal our land. God sees us together, even when he has to judge us when Achan sin God said all Israel have sin against me, when only one man had stolen that which was forbidden.

Joshua was given instruction concerning the next generation when they all was delivered. Most people believe that the opposite of Agape love is hate but in actuality, it is selfishness. In order to reach this next generation our focus must be placed on the Kingdom with the focus placed heavily on the King. The King gives directive and we obey. We do not take a vote on it we do gather to our political part to find out their beliefs we just obey. In the Kingdom when it comes to the laws morals and most everything the King establishes it. That anything he says he is now bound to it and anything he did not say he is not responsible for. Therefore, when people ask me about my thoughts concerning moral issues like homosexuality abortion I tell them I have none but I will tell you what the King said. This generation like the Greeks of old loves to argue politics and moral issues and reaching no conclusion believing their belief is just as worthy as yours. So move the discussion to the King and the Kingdom. God's word can stand alone needing no help from us.

Seeing us as one also helps us focus on removing unneeded division. Many of our young people are confused because there is so much division in the church. With all this division among us, why should they pick sides? Paul taught us that God is not the author of confusion but peace. There is power release in unity. Jesus said where two or three are gather in my name I will be in the midst. He said when you pray say our father. The Bible in the book of Acts tells that the people were in one place in one accord when the Holy Spirit fell.

Stories were told in 1906, when the Holy Spirit was poured out on Azusa Street in Los Angeles California, that they were together blacks, white, rich, poor seeking the face of God. There was a great out pouring of God's Spirit that the place would seem to be on fire at times. People heard unlearned people praying and praising God in a language not their own. One of the things this generation is fascinated with is experience. Most of the churches do not have the money, nor can the resources to give an experience like the world. However, the world cannot compete with the power of God. I have noticed when we are one there is very little we cannot do. The story of the Tower of Babel reinforced this. God said the people are one and there is nothing they cannot do. He had to intervene to divide them. Oneness is a necessity. In one of my meetings in Jamaica God gave a voiced to a young man who had never spoken, because we were one. We have seen the dead raised when the people were one. People who were tormented by evil spirits were released when the people were one.

So to see a move of God and give this generation the experience they long for we must operate as a Kingdom. This oneness is not only a spiritual truth but it works in the natural, how many sports team you have seen, not having the talent of other teams but yet come out victorious because they work together as one. I must say not one of my favorite teams but the New England Patriots is such a team. They do not always have the talent but coach somehow gets them to work as one and the result is championships. The Miami Dolphin team that still holds the record for an undefeated season were not filled with superstars but work together and did what no other have. The Bible tells us that the children of this world are wiser than the children of light. Time want permit me to talk about the successful business that work together for great wealth and success. This generation needs to hear the voice of God let us put aside our differences and work together as a Kingdom.

Teach the power of authority

God's instructions, God's man, and his men

Joshua 4: *When the whole nation had finished crossing the Jordan, the Lord said to Joshua, [2] "Choose twelve men from among the people, one from each tribe, [3] and tell them to take up twelve stones from the middle of the Jordan, from right where the priests are standing, and carry them over with you and put them down at the place where you stay tonight."*

      Authority a sign of faith: A Centurion man of great authority In Luke 7 came to Jesus for help. One must realize that another in authority does not diminish yours. People of authority embellished one another. Another of authority did not intimidate the Centurion who was a man of great authority. There are so many splits in the body of Christ because of selfish ambitions. This did not have low self-esteem because he knew who he was. Most who fight authority in the church or just in general have low self-esteem. Others will always see this even when you hid it in spirituality. First, we must understand that God gave man authority in Genesis 1:26 over everything but another man.

When man has authority over another man God must give it to him and the man must agree to it. God says submit to one another. Submission is not a sign of weakness but strength. Who is the strongest the horse or the rider? The horse is yet he places his strength under the rider to accomplish a goal.

The Centurion knew who he was and told Jesus he did. He said he was under authority and in authority. You will never be the kind of leader who can change a generation unto you are under and in authority. Iron sharpens iron. When the Centurion made his statement, Jesus responded as though he had not heard what he had said. The man gave a beautiful thesis on authority and Jesus responded with a thesis on faith. The Centurion said he was a man under authority and in authority; he said I tell this one to go and he goes I tell this one to come and he comes. Then he tells Jesus he did not have to come to his home just speak the word and his servant would be healed. After this, Jesus said I have not seen this kind of faith in all of Israel. This would be equivalent to him saying I found more faith in the world than I do in my church. The man received his miracle because of a faith that operates on speaking from a place of authority. We do not recognize the spiritual leader any more as anyone special. I know what some are thinking, some leaders have place themselves in some awful position so they do not deserve our submission. I would differ with you there. Saul was one of the most disobedient Kings God ever had but David respected the fact that in the past God had his hand on him and he should not touch him. Family authority did not originate with the man but from God so when I respected it I respect God.

In the book of Ezekiel 25 God is rebuking some nations and promising judgment on them. His complaint was not that his people were right but others said and did about what he had established. I would be very careful about what I say about God's leaders. The Lord says vengeance is mine I will repay. He says who are you to judge another man's servant. Here is my personal advice and believe it is from the Lord.

I would find a leader I could respect rather than stay complain and fight. Your whole earthly existent is tied to your spiritual leader. In third John we are told beloved I pray above all things that you would prosper and be in health even as you soul prosper. Notice that prosperity is tied to soul advancement not spirit. Therefore, to the same degree that my soul prospers I will prosper and be healed. I must discover how to get my soul to prosper because I desire to prosper.

The writer of the book of Hebrews gives me my answer. He tells me to obey those that have the rule over me for they watch for my soul. He says not to cause them grief because it would hinder my prosperity. Salvation is divided in threes. Three times past, present and future. Three things spirit, soul and body. Three agents, Jesus is over my spirit, my spiritual leader is over the soul, and I am over my flesh. When we misunderstand theology, we can live a disturbed life. You were saved (in your spirit), you are being saved (in your soul) and you shall be saved (in your body). Jesus is the High Priest over your spirit, your spiritual leader is responsible for your soul and you have the responsibility over your body. With all this in mind you can see how important it is to be submitted to Christ in your spirit and to be submitted to your leader in your soul and you die daily in your flesh. So many people are afraid to take communion on the fear of dying. They have been told if they have sin in their life and take communion that they could be sick or even die.

This is not what the passage in Corinthians teaches. This is dealing with not discerning his body, which would include authority. God started this mission of reaching the next generation by choosing leadership, First Joshua and then twelve men one from each tribe. If there is anything need to reach this next generation it is men and women who are in authority and under authority. God was so disturbed with the leadership in the past he did not speak on a consistent basis for over four hundred years. He only started talking regularly when Jesus a leader he could trust showed up. Jesus said he only did what he seen the father doing. I wonder how many of us that God has given spiritual parents only do what you see them doing or what you want to do. Let's set a good example before this generation of real Godly Authority. If we are told, twelve stones do not get eleven or even thirteen. Obedience is better than the sacrifice. You cannot come home and have roast pastor and change a generation.

Memories:

Joshua 4:3 and tell them to take up twelve stones from the middle of the Jordan, from right where the priests are standing, and carry them over with you and put them down at the place where you stay tonight. "God instructs Joshua to get some men to set up a memorial for the next generation. First, when you think memorial you must think memories. Our mind is one of the most powerful things on this earth. The mind can be very creative and intuitive but also devastating if not use properly. God warns us that as a man think so is he. So we become what we think. So memories can be positive or negative. Let's examine an instruction from Paul's writings. Philippians 4: [8] *Finally, brothers and sisters, whatever is true, whatever is noble, whatever is right, whatever is pure, whatever is lovely, whatever is admirable—if anything is excellent or praiseworthy—think about such things.* God through the Apostle instructs us on how to use our memory. First on the list is honesty or truth- so your memories should be impregnated with thoughts that were God inspired. Why be he declared himself to be the truth, let God be true and every man a liar. Next on the list is nobility or honor, the French say that nobility obligates you or that is to give the noble great responsibility. You memories must be consumed with the weight of responsibility God has given us as believers. What so ever things are right appears next in this list? Again, this would lead us back to what has been given us by God.

For the Bible says that Abraham believed God and it was counted unto him for righteousness. So our right stands hinges on our faith in God and not our abilities or works. Your memories must be filled with the memories of what God has provide for you that was impossible to obtain on your own. Now he tells us to think on purity. Purity is absents of any other alloy. That means you are trusting God and God alone for your future. When you face problems, you only look to him for the answer. Lovely or desirable is next. What our minds focus on is not our problems but the desired things. Things like our love for Christ our love for others and answered prayer. What is that you admire are the things you focus on are is it the problems you hate that get most of your time. Last, our thoughts should be filled with things that would bring praise to our God. These are the things God tells us to focus on not let our minds run wild and keep us in fear or doubt, but things that are healthy for you and will bless the next generation.

  Paul tells us in another passage to let our Christ mind be in you. He did not say let your mind be like Christ but to allow Christ mind to be in you. What was his mind he knew who he was he did not think he was committing robbery to think as he did but gave way to humility rather than pride. Knowing who you are is not a badge to do as you will but as he will. With these thoughts in mind, let us return to God's instruction to Joshua. He was to choose twelve men to carry out this task. It might sound simple to us now but I am sure it was not a simple thing then. First, they were to go where they dreaded. Then bring out a memorial and the place it where they sleep.

  In light of this, let us look at this through our eyes. God has just delivered you from a life threatening experience, Cancer, Divorce, loss of a love one, heart attack, enough you get the picture. Now he tells you to revisit the event and bring something out of it to use to show future generations what happen. That means in a real way you go back through your problem again and keep and everlasting memorial for others. Next, you are to set the memorial up where you sleep. Look at this a constant reminder of what you been through and place it where you rest. Rest or sleep is the one place you go to forget the problems of today now there is a reminder when you get up and when you go to bed. We will look at this a little closer later but now just to say that God does this because he has taught us how to think and dwelling on the problem is not it. Even in our prayers, we sometimes are guilty of focusing in on the wrong thing our problems. He told us whatsoever you desire when you pray believe you receive them and you shall have them.

Uniqueness of this memorial

Only people with strength can carry these stones. I am not just talking about physical strength but also spiritual strength. We all know that it is not by power nor by might but by my spirit says the Lord. Only those that have totally submitted to the Holy Spirit can carry this kind of memory. The memories of a close to death experience and not focus on the negative but the possible. Joseph was a man he experience many near death experiences and yet his view was positive. To be sold by your own brothers after being placed in a dry pit. To be lied on by your employers wife and thrown in prison. To help someone else get out and forgotten by them for years. Yet after the death of his father and the brothers or now sure he is going to kill them. However, listen how Joseph handle it. *Genesis 50:* [15] *When Joseph's brothers saw that their father was dead, they said, "What if Joseph holds a grudge against us and pays us back for all the wrongs we did to him?"* [16] *So they sent word to Joseph, saying, "Your father left these instructions before he died:* [17] *'This is what you are to say to Joseph: I ask you to forgive your brothers the sins and the wrongs they committed in treating you so badly.' Now please forgive the sins of the servants of the God of your father." When their message came to him, Joseph wept.* [18] *His brothers then came and threw themselves down before him. "We are your slaves," they said.* [19] *But Joseph said to them, "Do not be afraid. Am I in the place of God?* [20] *You intended to harm me, but God intended it for good to accomplish what is now being done, the saving of many lives.* [21] *So then, do not be afraid. I will provide for you and your children." And he reassured them and spoke kindly to them.*

Joseph understood what Paul taught us in the New Testament back then. All things work together for good for those who love God and called according to his purpose. Joseph had reached his destiny and that led him down a few roads he would have like to avoid. However, these were necessary roads to prepare him for the throne. He did not live in la la land; he knew that purpose was to destroy him but God had a greater plan. Had they not did as they did he would not had been in Egypt and if not there not available to Pharaoh and not him the people of Egypt would have suffer for greater than they did and Israel could have been Annihilated. So to have a testimony that will change the next generation will take the strength of this generation.

In addition, to change the next generation you had to be a burden barer. They had to carry these stones on their shoulders. This reminds me of the High Priest dress. He had twelve stones over his heart and six on each shoulder. The stones represented the tribes of Israel. Notice first they were precious stones. Until we see the next generation is precious, we will not sacrifice for them. They were to be on the Priest heart before God. When was the last time you went in before God for someone of the next generation on your heart? They were to also bare them on their shoulders. Let us examine another Pauline passage. Galatians 6:1 Brothers and sisters, if someone is caught in a sin, you who live by the spirit should restore that person gently. However, watch yourselves, or you also may be tempted. ²Carry each other's burdens, and in this way, you will fulfill the law of Christ.

The stones they were carrying were not for them but for the next generation. We will extend ourselves for ourselves but what about someone who may not even exist at the time you are told to carry the burden. Some of those children were not yet born but they were told to carry the burden. They were also were to know that this would be a sign. A sign does many things. A sign can show you the right direction it can also warn of danger. These stones were to do both point them to God for help and show what can happen if they do not. What kind of sign are you? My mother wanted me to know the severity of the call of God on my life. She would tell me these words as a warning to me. "Son, you will sometimes be the only Bible that some people will read. Then she would say what will they read? Sobering question since God tells us through Apostle Peter something about us.

1 Peter 2: Therefore, rid yourselves of all malice and all deceit, hypocrisy, envy, and slander of every kind. ² Like newborn babies, crave pure spiritual milk, so that by it you may grow up in your salvation, ³ now that you have tasted that the Lord is good.

The Living Stone and a Chosen People

⁴ As you come to him, the living Stone—rejected by humans but chosen by God and precious to him— ⁵ you also, like living stones, are being built into a spiritual house[a] to be a holy priesthood, offering spiritual sacrifices acceptable to God through Jesus Christ. ⁶ For in Scripture it says: "See, I lay a stone in Zion, a chosen and precious cornerstone, and the one who trusts in him will never be put to shame."[b]⁷ Now to you who believe, this stone is precious. But to those who do not believe,"The stone the builders rejected has become the cornerstone,"[c]⁸ and,"A stone that causes people to stumble and a rock that makes them fall."[d]

They stumble because they disobey the message—which is also, what they were destined for. We are told that we are living stones so living signs to the next generation. We are warned in the first part of this chapter to remove everything that would cause us to fall as well as those who follow us. The main stone will be the reason some will make it and some will fall. Christ is also a stone to some a stone of blessing and direction as those stones Joshua was told to put up. Jesus is also a stone of offense to those who reject him. So we do not have the obligation to win the world but to witness to it to be a good sign.

Kingship Examination

- What was the sign Joshua was instructed to remove from Jordan?
    1. A Tree
    2. A fish
    3. Stones
    4. Ark
- In Luke 7 Jesus taught faith and the student talked about
    1. Love
    2. Authority
    3. Peace
    4. Joy
- What was the purpose of the stones?
    1. To build a house
    2. To remember what God did
    3. To build a Temple
    4. Protection from the enemy
- They were to place the stones
    1. Everywhere they traveled
    2. Where they slept
    3. In the Temple

4. All the above

- The stones was to remind
    1. The next generation
    2. Their enemies
    3. The Elders
    4. Joshua

- The memorial would cause them to focus on
    1. How deep the Jordan was
    2. The wind and waves
    3. Their salvation
    4. The pain of the trip

- Only people with great _____ can carry these stones
    1. Wisdom
    2. Insight
    3. Intelligence
    4. Strength

- Peter called us
    1. Champions
    2. Strong men
    3. Living stones
    4. Church people

King to do list

- Unite with a Christian fellowship

- Ask the leader to be your mentor or recommend one

- Ask for a weekly to do list: example, prayer, Bible reading, witnessing, giving include tithe, and personal assignments from your mentor

- Setup memorial- keep a journal of God's victories for you

Chapter Seven
Breaking Curses

I know that this might sound foreign to so many. This may sound like something from the dark ages but believe me there are curses attached to our family that prevent us from going forward. If we are to reach the next generation, we need to break the curse off our families. There are so many kinds of curses it would be impossible for this book to address them all. I will first deal with my family and me. Raised in a Christian home with a father who was a minister of the gospel and a mother who was a domestic missionary. When I arrived on this earth, the church was already a part of my life. I was in church all day Sunday, mid-week service prayer meeting, my mother's choir rehearsal, and when old enough my own rehearsal. We had family members who had fruit trees and I loved a particular fruit. I was not allowed go to their home without my father. This side of the family practiced witchcraft at least that is what they told me. I thought my parents had lost their minds, witchcraft please. There were other traits that I observed later as my eyes were opened that were something that my family was controlled by. There were certain kinds of sickness that was consistent in my family. I can hear you now saying that was just your DNA. I do know that your DNA plays apart in these things but here is another answer also.

There are other traits in my family, many of the men were handsome and admired by women and the feeling was mutual. This caused a strain on marriages and sometimes led to divorce. I was a victim and willing participant in this last one. At the age of eighteen, I moved away from home. I stayed with a relative for about two months. I then moved out on my own. I met a young woman through her sister that worked with me. She was a nice girl brought up in the country and as far as I know, was loyal to me. However, when I got into the work environment I began to experience things I was not ready to handle. That was attention from the opposite sex and I liked it. I began cheating on my wife. Then girls voluntarily began to give me money. This is when another vice entered my life: pimping. I got involved in this life style. I also began to do what I once hated, drugs. I was first exposed to drugs by being in the car with a relative and his friends. Then they got in a car and began shooting drugs, I will never forget my reaction I was scared to death. The next time I had an experience with drugs another of my cousin's returned from the arm forces snorting cocaine up a dollar bill. I disowned him. Because this spirit was in my family, I was soon enticed and eventually it possessed me. In the end, I was not only doing drugs, I was also a drug dealer.

  I hope I will not lose you but now I will take you in a world I can only thank God that I am no longer involved in. Drugs opened the door to other worlds that I did not know existed, the spirit world. I will explain to you that drugs are a doorway into the occult. The devil really tries to stay and manipulate from the background but when you use drugs, he gets bolder. He does this because many will blame what they cannot explain on their drug use. As far as sex goes, I met and was using a girl for my own gain. Later I found out that she was actually using me. In her attempt to be number one and control me, she had secured the help of a witch. I was sure this was by the instruction of the witch and the greed that was in my heart she found a way into my home. When I arrived at her home on one of my many visits, she had a bust of a man sitting on her coffee table. I love art so I complimented her taste. She responded by saying baby, do you really like it. I replied yes I do. She then told me just take it with you and I did. I was not aware of the power of amulets.

  Things that have been dedicated to the work of darkness, but this was exactly what this was. After this time, I realized I had abilities that were beyond the natural world. I could read minds I could tell a person their zodiac sign without their input. I had a dog that I named Lucifer and I could communicate with him without opening my mouth. I was in martial art and could kick a ceiling and return to my feet. Before these and other powers showed up, I was at a club where two men were auguring. I stood and watched. The man was about six foot four inches tall and about two hundred and twenty-five pounds and the other was about five foot eight and one hundred and thirty pounds. The bigger man boasted that he was going to knock the little man out. To which the little man very unafraid said you are not. He went on to say I now control you and you cannot move your arms. I stood in amazement as the big man struggled to move his arms. Eventually he cried and begged the little man to turn him loose. I want you to know that the smaller man never touched him he just spoke. The smaller man asked him, if I let you go do you think you will act right? He said yes and could then move his arms. When this event ended the smaller man, turned to me and said you have this power too.

Later I discovered I did. I used it to manipulate girls for my benefit. Physic teaches that once something gains momentum it can only be stop by a greater force. This is what happened to me and is the reason I am telling you this story. I was eating at a certain restaurant in my city and saw a picture of some girls. They were a group called Sweet Spirit, they were singing at this placed called the Adam's Apple, I decided to go and see what they were about. Three things got my attention first they were beautiful girls, second their name had spirit in it they must be aware and thirdly my love for music and thinking this was a secular group. I went on the wrong night was invited in to a prayer meeting. It was there that something greater than me stopped my momentum. God spoke to me in an audible voice. He said it was not an accident that I was there, he arranged it, and this was my last opportunity. I began to cry and so did some men who were with me for my protection. They at the time were just doing what they saw me do. The curse began to break that night. This was a Wednesday night, Thursday night I went to the church associated with this coffee house and Friday returned to the coffee house for the original reason I went to the concert. Saturday I attended prayer meeting. Sunday went to both morning and evening services, Monday I signed up and began Bible College. While in school, we had a visitor from Africa that was a guest in the church and came to speak to our class. He spoke about amulets and their power, this was a revelation to me. This bust came and was suspended in the air in front of me I knew what that meant.

This was one of the enemies' amulets. I was just newly saved and afraid to go home. Because of my past life, some of the residuals such as a nice apartment and furniture caused my house to be one of the places that my classmates loved to visit. Therefore, I knew I would have help when facing something that terrifying to me. But this day no one was available to go home with me and I would have to face my demons alone. I found out later my classmates were facing some of their own. One group who were rooming together went home to destroy an Ouija board. They told the story about how the board did not want to be destroyed, so it leaped from the table and ran around the room making sounds like a pig. They were successful in catching it and destroying it. I went home with my mindset on destroying this bust. I was so afraid but I took it in the ally, took an ax, and tried to break it in pieces unsuccessfully.

Finally with little resolve and less exertion than in the past, I brought the ax down one more time, said in the name of Jesus and it shattered into many pieces. The only way I can describe what happened next is to say I felt like a butterfly coming out of its cocoon. Save prior to this I was but, I was not free. I had much fear surrounding my life up until this time. I feel these sequences of events helped me break the curses off my life. When faced with continual problems or events, it can be the result of a curse. Curse defined: (Noun) a prayer or invocation for harm or injury to come upon one; evil or misfortune that comes as if in response to imprecation or as retribution; a cause of great harm or misfortune. (verb) to use profanely insolent language against, blaspheme; to call upon divine or supernatural power to send injury upon; to execrate in fervent and often profane terms; to bring great evil upon, to afflict.

First, know that the price of your redemption has been paid in full. Galatians 3: [13] *Christ redeemed us from the curse of the law by becoming a curse for us, for it is written: "Cursed is everyone who is hung on a pole."*[h] [14] *He redeemed us in order that the blessing given to Abraham might come to the Gentiles through Christ Jesus, so that by faith we might receive the promise of the spirit'.*

I think it is ironic that God by the Holy Spirit which I do not believe is an accident uses the thirteenth verse to describe our freedom the very number so many have given to the devil and are superstitious about. Christ himself believed in and became a curse to redeem us from the curse. Redemption has to do with a purchase. We sold our selves into sin and over to the devil and thereby his curses. However, Christ by his death on the cross paid the price of redemption. Not only to keep you from hell but also from hells effects on earth. The curses come because of our tie with sin and the devil. Once you have been born again, you operate under new authority and power. Notice Christ redeemed us from the curse that you might operate under the blessings of Abraham. So what are blessings of Abraham? Do you know why knowing the blessings of Abraham so important? Because if you do not know where you are, you can become content, being saved but still operate under the curse.

Genesis 12: *The LORD had said to Abram, "Go from your country, your people and your father's household to the land I will show you.* [2] *"I will make you into a great nation, and I will bless you; I will make your name great, and you will be a blessing.* [a]3 *I will bless those who bless you, and whoever curses you I will curse; and all peoples on earth will be blessed through you".*

First, the blessing of Abraham means you are separated

from what you know and taken on an adventure. Secondly, you observe what and where the Lord shows you. The next thing on God's agenda is the making of a Kingdom not just a home or a church. God is about Kingdom building. God next declared you blessed with a purpose to be a blessing. You will recognize people who join to your purpose and those who bless you become blessed. In addition, anyone who tries to stop the purpose of God in your life will find himself or herself under a curse. God promised us his protection from the enemy. Isaiah 54: ¹⁷ No weapon that is formed against thee shall prosper; and every tongue that shall rise against thee in judgment thou shalt condemn. This is the heritage of the servants of the LORD, and their righteousness is of me, saith the LORD.

One must understand he did not promise a weapon free environment, but these weapons would not be successful against us. When someone places a curse on you, they must speak it. God gave us defense. When tongues speak against you, you are to condemn it. That means to send it back to its origin, Hell. When you condemn something, you send it to hell. Now notice something else about the blessing, it is to be worldwide in its scope. In a sort of tongue and cheek way I asked my people how many of you are still in sin? They have been around me long enough to know exactly what I am talking about. I asked how many of them have a passport; if they say they do not I tell them that they are in sin. Jesus told us to go into the entire world and preach and without a passport, you cannot obey. So I now ask you, how many of you are still in sin?

The other part of Abraham's blessings is in Genesis 15: *After these things the word of the LORD came unto Abram in a vision, saying, Fear not, Abram: I am thy shield, and thy exceeding great reward. ² And Abram said, LORD God, what wilt thou give me, seeing I go childless, and the steward of my house is this Eliezer of Damascus? ³ And Abram said, Behold, to me thou hast given no seed: and, lo, one born in my house is mine heir. ⁴ And, behold, the word of the LORD came unto him, saying, This shall not be thine heir; but he that shall come forth out of thine own bowels shall be thine heir. ⁵ And he brought him forth abroad, and said, look now toward heaven, and tell the stars, if thou be able to number them: and he said unto him, so shall thy seed be. ⁶ And he believed in the* LORD; *and he counted it to him for righteousness.*

Another reason we are safe from the enemy's attacks is that God promised us he would protect us. David felt so safe, that he said even if death surrounds, me I would have no fear because of God's presence. If there is, only one thing you should know for sure that should be the presence of God is with you. There is nothing so powerful than to know the presence of God. I shared my testimony earlier and told you about the things I could do, and that is why so many people are sucked in to the devil's web. The other side of the story is the fear that overtakes you. I lived in constant fear because the devil's mission not only includes you but also is against you. I heard a woman from England who now is a minister of the gospel tell her story. She had been a witch for many years and had personal contact with Satan.

He had appeared to her many times and walked through barn fires with her. She had the ability to kill a bird in flight and to make her whole coven invisible. Standing on a street, she saw people going a hall to church. She decided to go in and hit the preacher. When she arrived in the meeting, they were praising God with a song most of us heard in Sunday school. The song was yes Jesus love me. She sat there amazed because all of the times she had been in Satan's presence he had never told her he loved her. She decided after the message to go forward and give her life to Christ. When she would get up something would knock her back down. It took her a long time to get there but she finally made it. Like most of us, the devil tricks us into thinking that we have this special power or aura around us she had been deceived. The people in this meeting knew what to do and cast out forty-eight demons. Demons are spirits without a body and are always in search of one. The Bible seems to teach that they are in torment without a body. We have study earlier that God gave man authority on the earth and if you are not in a body, you have none. These demons in their quest to rule from your life often torment the one possessed. That is why so many people who have been in the occult end up in mental wards. However, being a child of Abraham by faith we have God's promise of protection.

God also promised us that we would have heirs. First, an heir is a useless commodity if there is nothing to leave them. So just the promise of an heir is proof that God also want to bless you. It is the will of God for you to be blessed. Remember the scripture we studied earlier the writer said "I pray above all things that you prosper and be in health."

With this in mind except the Lord, build the house we labor in vain. Abraham had desired a family without any success. Nevertheless, when God intervened he brought forth laughter (Isaac). God promised the Kingdom would be innumerable. Therefore, saint of God you have nothing to worry about the curse that the enemy sent I love this scripture proverb 26: [2] As the bird by wandering, as the swallow by flying, so the curse causeless shall not come.

God removes the fear from our heart with the promise that no curse shall come without a cause. Therefore, we have to remove any chance for the curse. One curse can come and descend on us just by being born in a family. I can hear someone saying this is not fair but the blessing of God comes on us for just being born again in his family. We must denounce the evil practices of our family. Another source of curses comes by soul ties. I recommend a great book for dealing with these curses and many others. The book is Prayer Passport, by Dr. Daniel Olukoya. You will probably have to order it online.

The reason the devil gets away with so much in our lives is that we just do not know. Not knowing does not eliminate the pain and heartache the curse brings. Hosea 4: [6] "My people are destroyed for lack of knowledge: because thou hast rejected knowledge, I will also reject thee, that thou shalt be no priest to me: seeing thou hast forgotten the law of thy God, I will also forget thy children". You cannot blame our church or our pastor when we have a Bible at home that we do not read. I am not letting us pastors off the hook we should educate our people. However, a lot of this teaching takes time and will bring ridicule to the teacher. Like all of you, pastors want to be liked. God teaches that not having knowledge can destroy us. It also causes us to live a rejected life. It is one thing to have people to reject you but to be rejected by God is another. I hear people make the statement with great enthusiasm that knowledge is power. I am convinced just knowing does not empower you, but once you apply what you know you become powerful. I think I must also mention that not knowing does not eliminate the consequences of spiritual laws just as it does not with natural laws. You not knowing that a wire is live will not stop the shock when you touch it.

Ignorance results are dependable

One of my favorite uncles, Luzell Bolden, use to tell us growing up that ignorance is a terrible thing. I know he was using this to motivate us to study hard. However, the way and how he said it always brought laughter. However, as I grew and reflected back on his words I was amazed at his wisdom. My father, his brother Willie Bolden Jr., would say that I would visit fools hill, and then I would have understanding. Boy were they both right. I did discover that ignorance is a terrible thing and I did visit fools hill. I discovered I was not the only one who had checked in to fools hill. When studying at Indiana University extension in Fort Wayne Indiana, I was young and already knew everything, so I wasted a lot of my time getting high before coming to class. When one of my professors, a woman for the life of me, I cannot remember her name, but I will never forget one of her counseling sessions with me. She was a white woman this is only important because the message she gave me was important. She called me by my full name and said you are a very intelligent young man. Then these words came but you are wasting your time. This was when things in this country was a lot worse than they are now.

If you study the history of Indiana, at one time the Klan ran the government from the Governor right on down. She said do you see that white student sitting next to you? I said I did. She said to get the same job he will get with a C; you will need to make an A. She was telling me again what I had learned from my uncle and my father. That was you on fool's hill and that ignorance is a terrible thing. O yes I finally got myself together and left fools hill. I found what my purpose was, I went on and graduated college and continued to get other graduate degrees. I am glad that was finally behind me but there was other thing I was still ignorant of, the things of the Kingdom of God.

First, I need to turn the helm of my life over to Christ. I am happy to say I did that. However, that was just the beginning I need more knowledge. I know that a lot of us grew up in churches where we did not get the proper training and sometimes the wrong training. I remember a guest pastor came to our Sunday school class. We were excited to have a pastor teaching our class, this would be great. In one of his illustrations, he said I hold this and no one can change my mind, and then he repeated that with emphasis. We could not wait to hear this spiritual truth. He said "a man should not treat his girlfriend better than he treats his wife". WOW! Some of us were shock and others were saying amen. Once I went to a pastor for some advice. I was now a pastor and was facing something at the time I did not know how to handle. The problem was a young woman who had joined my church and had decided she wanted to have sex with me and told me as much. I explained that I was happily married and this was not the lifestyle I wanted. Nevertheless, that only lit a match to her pursuit.

The pastor I went to for advice, told me "that I was a man first and that there was nothing wrong with me going outside of my marriage". Again, WOW! In both those cases were men who were my seniors who I had respect for until then. I could easily have taken their advice and told God that this is what I learned from my superiors. However, would I be free of judgment because of my ignorance?

Let us examine this scripture. Leviticus 5: [17] "And if a soul sin, and commit any of these things which are forbidden to be done by the commandments of the LORD; though he wist it not, yet is he guilty, and shall bear his iniquity".

The King James word wist is saying you did not know. So God is saying in spite of the fact you do not know and stand in ignorance you will still be judge by the commandment. Remember the scripture. God conceals and Kings search for revelation.

Knowledge like ignorance is consistent

Knowledge the opposite of ignorance gets opposite results. We know that ignorance brings us under the judgment for that I did not know. So what does knowledge do? *Isaiah 27:* [11] *"When the boughs thereof are withered, they shall be broken off: the women come, and set them on fire: for it is a people of no understanding: therefore he that made them will not have mercy on them, and he that formed them will shew them no favor".*

This scripture teaches us that ignorant people will not have God's mercy or his favor. The opposite is true for the knowledgeable. We shall have God's mercy and his favor. I have discovered in my walk with God how much I need them both. Knowledge does not prevent me from failure and falling short (sin). I with all my knowledge of God and his Kingdom principles still fall short. It is not the will of God to destroy anyone. We choose to disobey or not even learn his principles. Which cause us to fall on the level of beings that hell was prepared for Satan and his angels. Repentance will cause God to be merciful to us because he knows that we are only clay. The other benefit lost by ignorance is favor. I heard someone say that favor is not fair. I would like to say over my many years of receiving his favor you could be right that it is not fair but sure is a lot of fun. Listen to Psalms 6:4 "Return, O LORD, deliver my soul: oh save me for thy mercies' sake". Many have been delivered by mercy why not you? Psalms 25:6 "Return, O LORD, deliver my soul: oh save me for thy mercies' sake". God turns back to you due to mercy. When you are about to give up hear the voice of David and follow these instructions. According to Psalms 103:2, "Bless the LORD, O my soul, and forget not all his benefits": This is where the knowledge comes in the more you know about God the more you will trust him. For as the songwriter wrote "he keeps on doing great things for me".

The Holy Spirit a consistent guide into truth

In closing this chapter, I want us to focus on the helper God has given us. We are such blessed people to live in this season. I know that there are people that wished they could have been on earth when Moses were here and still others would have liked to walked the streets of Jerusalem with Jesus. I would like to impress upon your heart that this is the greatest time to be alive. I see three divisions of God's work upon this earth, first the time of the Father during Moses' time, he was for us but we could not draw near him. Jesus was there walking, talking and performing miracles upon this earth, how exciting. You would either have had to been one of the disciples or in the vicinity where he traveled. You and I live in the time of the work of the Holy Spirit he is the presence of the Father and the Son and he now lives in us, what a blessing. There is hidden knowledge that needs to be interpreted for us.

John 16: [12] *"I have yet many things to say unto you, but ye cannot bear them now.* [13] *Howbeit when he, the Spirit of Truth, is come, he will guide you into all truth: for he shall not speak of himself; but whatsoever he shall hear, that shall he speak: and he will shew you things to come.* [14] *He shall glorify me: for he shall receive of mine, and shall shew it unto you.* [15] *All things that the Father hath are mine: therefore said I, that he shall take of mine, and shall shew it unto you"*.

Jesus told his disciples that were not yet able to understand the knowledge he had. Another would come after him that would explain it to them. He called him the Spirit of Truth. He would be a guide to us in truth. He said that he would not come to talk about himself but make Jesus known to us. Whatever he receives from Jesus he would make it know unto us. Jesus said all things belong to the Father was his and that the Holy Spirit would make it known unto us. There are so many things that we are completely ignorant of, but the Holy Spirit will make it known. I was preaching one Sunday when a young man was responding by saying amen to everything I said. This is not unusual; we are very emotional in our worship and our response to the word of God. The Holy Spirit made me aware that this was not him but another spirit. Therefore, I stopped preaching, took authority over the spirit, and returned to preaching. Not only did the young man be quite but got up and left. After the service, many of the members were confused and came to tell me so. They said this man was saying amen and not doing anything wrong. I tried to explain to them why I did it and left it alone.

The next Sunday the young man returned, jumped up, karate kicked the door, and everyone knew. I was preaching in Trinidad and discerned by the spirit that most of the choir was demon possessed. I went into the choir loft and it was pandemonium. I cast demons out a long time before I could preach. I was in Paris France preaching and can still remember what I was preaching. I was preaching on the Holy Spirit and when I finished I came down to pray for those in attendance. I would solicit first the help of the Elders of the church to help when I discerned by the Holy Spirit that most of them were demon possessed. The Holy Spirit will guide you into unknown knowledge. He not only does this but he is our early warning system. I will not say God will use you in the same way he does me, but when I need to pray for someone, I will see that person's face on other people all day until I pray for them. I do not have the time, space or the knowledge to tell you how many ways he brings us knowledge, but just know this he does. He alarms me when I am in trouble or about to sin.

There are people that the Holy Spirit has worked on their heart for salvation and he will lead you to them. The Holy Spirit is so important to the work of the ministry you and I cannot do the work without him. I heard one of the great preachers of our time, who also leads one of the largest churches in the world say that he used to leave a chair vacant by him on the platform to remind himself that he did not do the work alone. When he would arise to preach he would look to the chair and say come on Holy Ghost. In closing, I remember a funeral that I had to do. A young woman in my church was murdered. I thought I cannot do this I am too weak, but when I stood to preach all of the weakness had subsided and grew to strength. I preached with the help of the spirit and many came to know the Lord. Please quit working for the Lord and work with Him.

Kingship Examination

Continual problems could be the result of a curse

1. True
2. False

Drugs can play a part in the occult

1. True
2. False

Galatians 3 teaches we are

1. Under a curse
2. To place curses on others
3. Redeemed from the curse
4. None of the above

Curses are because of sin and the Devil

1. True
2. False

We were blessed with Abraham Genesis 12, 15 Galatians 3

1. True
2. False

God promise to protect us in Isaiah 54

1. True
2. False

Ignorance gives the enemy the advantage over us (Hosea 4:6)

1. True
2. False

Curses still comes ignorant or not (Leviticus 5:17)

1. True
2. False

King to do list

- Know that the curse is broken (Galatians 3)
- Study the blessings (Genesis 12,15)
- Close doors to the enemy (drugs, astrology, sin and all works of darkness)
- Get pray for deliverance
- Remove things from your home that gives the devil access
- Get friends that will help you stay strong
- Faithfully attend church services, Bible study and prayer meeting
- Study the word daily (Hosea 4:6, Leviticus 5:17)

Chapter Eight

Building Successfully

While reaching this next generation you like the great Apostle Paul and Jesus himself must see yourself as a wise master builder. There are principles that must be adhered to reach our goals. These principles will work if you are building a life, business or church. One of the first things you need is a blue print. Since we are dealing primarily with Kingdom building we must start with God's blue print the Bible. Utilize the knowledge you have of the person. The Bible tells us to know those that labor among you. You also need the input of others.

This will sound strange to some but you need to do a background check. You are not doing this to hinder or to hold the person's past against them. This is to know where you can use them. Even if this person has repented and loves God with all their heart, you cannot put an ex-child molester with little children. This would hurt them by placing them around too much temptation and place the children in danger and set you up for a lawsuit. With these things in mind let us examine the scriptures for Godly principles.

Spiritual Truth: Synergy

As I was saying in the intro to this chapter, you need the help of others. Ezra 3: 1 *"And when the seventh month was come, and the children of Israel were in the cities, the people gathered themselves together as one man to Jerusalem"*. When Israel was still under bondage they were able to do great things because of synergy. They came together to rebuild The Temple, the walls and their city. In the New Testament Paul made a powerful statement, he said one man planted another man waters and God gives the increase. So we do need one another to carry out a successful mission on this earth. We must start thinking Kingdom and not just church. The Kingdom is much larger than the church and has many more able helpers than what we possess in our churches. We need to solicit the help of all of them. If they come to your church and has special needs that your church are not able to accommodate, why not suggest a church that has what these people need. There are churches in the Kingdom that utilize the arts or music or preaching style different from mine and this person is in search of a ministry like this why not recommend them there.

When I started ministry many years back, we were told to meet the banker of your town and attorney the city council people. We met the leaders and shakers of our town. You will never know when you will have need of them. I had a good relationship with my banker but found him to be prejudice against pastors. I went to borrow monies to build a new church he told me about all the pastors who had defaulted on their loans. I told him that I would build the church and would send him an invitation, this happen because I did not stop building relations. I was playing golf with a man I did not know, he ask my career I told him I was a pastor proudly. He asks me what was on my agenda for the church. I told him we had outgrown our facility and was looking to build another. He asks about the finances, I told him I had sought financing at my bank and they would loan me only enough to fail. He went father and ask what my plans were now. I told him I had prayed on it and were going to a bank around the corner. To which he said that is a brilliant idea I serve as the head of that banks board. To make a long story short we got the loan and build the building. To God be the Glory for leading me to that relationship. You are not an Island you need the help of others. The other scripture that brings this to light is in *Acts 2: "And when the day of Pentecost was fully come, they were all with one accord in one place.² And suddenly there came a sound from heaven as of a rushing mighty wind, and it filled all the house where they were sitting".*

I want you to notice three things that happen in these verses two of them were of God the one man. One was timing, when preparation meets opportunity you get great results. It was a season of harvest on the earth and also their preparation cause God to move from heaven. They obeyed God and were waiting together. This resulted in a great move of God. A group of people who will put away their differences and trust God together will not be stop. When I graduated Bible College and started the church in Fort Wayne, Indiana we had an unstoppable team of people. We hit the streets we went in bars we witness and sought the face of God together. We were amazed at the growth of the church. We would have hundreds of people gather at five am every morning for prayer, we would have noon prayer.

People from all walks of life were turning to God. There was one case where there were three and some four generations of prostitutes being saved. We had attorneys and doctors. My personal physician joined our church and I ask him why; he said because of the change he saw in me. The president of the city council was a member; there were professors from the universities there, the head of the board of works. There were also janitors factory workers, secretaries, there were people who drove six hours to be a part of the church. Every week between twenty and fifty people join our church. This was because a group of people had the same vision and God and the favor and timing of God. We closed down bars and closed a whole area to prostitutes. The Mayor of the city came and personally said the crime rate is way down because of the work of this church. The people were one and had a mind to work. We did the same thing in Tampa; Florida God gave me a team of people with a mind to work. We reached hundreds of people. We shut down prostitute motels and crack houses. We would walk and pray over our community for five days at five am and return on Saturday to witness. We had such an impact on the community that the crack dealers call the police on us. They could not do their business because of the attention we got. We called ourselves a Na-tional church, meaning one church many nations. We had at one time over fourteen nations attending our church. So at five o'clock am you have blacks white, Spanish and many other groups walking, this put fear in those with illegal business. There was a place that needed to be torn down. I had been to the city for its removal to no avail.

God spoke and said get some of the people and walk around it and pray and he would do something. We were told to do it for seven days on the third day people in hard hats were there. The old place was torn down. We walked and prayed silently. Yet after it was over a wine O came and said he had seen what we did, laughed and said do not walk around his house.

This next passage we will explore is where a lot of scholars believe the races were developed. *Genesis 11: "And the whole earth was of one language, and of one speech. ² And it came to pass, as they journeyed from the east, that they found a plain in the land of Shinar; and they dwelled there. ³ And they said one to another, Go to, let us make brick, and burn them thoroughly. And they had brick for stone, and slime had they for morter.⁴ And they said, Go to, let us build us a city and a tower, whose top may reach unto heaven; and let us make us a name, lest we be scattered abroad upon the face of the whole earth. ⁵ And the LORD came down to see the city and the tower, which the children of men builded. ⁶ And the LORD said, Behold, the people is one, and they have all one language; and this they begin to do: and now nothing will be restrained from them, which they have imagined to do. ⁷ Go to, let us go down, and there confound their language, that they may not understand one another's speech. ⁸ So the LORD scattered them abroad from thence upon the face of all the earth: and they left off to build the city. ⁹ Therefore is the name of it called Babel; because the LORD did there confound the language of all the earth: and from thence did the LORD scatter them abroad upon the face of all the earth."*

One of the things the devil has been very successful at is to keep the church divided by color. The most segregated place in America is church on Sunday morning. We will use every excuse in the world to remain so. We can point to atrocities that the other race has done and it is true. We can point to culture and the differences that we have and we do. If you really read this passage God did not divide us because of skin color. Skin color was not the issue but rebellion was. Man was doing all he could to resist the command of God to populate the earth. I believe that the many languages developed by God kept us apart and skin was a protection from the elements. But look at this when we were one as man not divide God himself testified that they are one and there is nothing they cannot do. I believe that like the many gifts and talents there are in the church. I believe that each race has something to offer the other that would enrich both. When I study church history and especially the Azusa Street movement I notice that the church was stronger because of unity. I believe when Shem, Ham and Japheth, these were the sons of Noah that populated this new earth, comes together we will be a force for the devil to deal with. William Seymour a partially blind black man started a prayer meeting in Los Angeles California many races assemble to receive what God was doing. Some of the first white pastors were ordain by Charles mason the Bishop of the Church of God in Christ.

One of those organizations was the Assembly of God; this took place around the turn of the century about 2006. It took the Assembly sixty years before the first black minister was ordained by them. So the white and black church separated from each other taking something that the other need. The white church was organized and had great teaching. The black church was very expressive in their emotion in worship and powerful preaching. So one was partially dried up why the other partially blew up. But if Shem (the Jews) with their rich history and understanding of the Torah and Shem (Caucasians) with organization and promotion and Ham (The Dark races) with his putting all he has in worship music and preaching and awesome prayer meetings would unite the devil would have no place to hide. Somehow if the Church of Jesus Christ could put down their differences and unite for Kingdom building.

Time want allow me to deal with the separation because of denomination. Of course ours will be the only one in heaven. OH how the devil has tricked us. God tells us through the great Apostle Paul that he is not the author of confusion but peace. We have everything else but peace. We can bring this down to the local church and you will find this same division. The deacons and the pastors, this group against that group, not to mention just this person not liking the other one. When I was growing up in Alabama, when we had iceboxes not refrigerators to preserve things for a long time my father had a smoke house and use salt to preserve the meat. He would incase the meat in the salt and it would keep it from spoiling. God call us the salt of the earth that means we are to bring protection to the earth and preserve it. But with all this division it is an impossible job. They tell me that the two most important components of salt are sodium and chlorine, both which are deadly when taken separately. The devil in his quest to stop the plan of God is always trying to break us down into sodium and chlorine that rather than preserve life we destroy it. Lack of agreement makes it impossible to get anything accomplished. The reward is greater when we work together. Ecclesiastes 4: *[8]"There is one alone, and there is not a second; yea, he hath neither child nor brother: yet is there no end of all his labour; neither is his eye satisfied with riches; neither saith he, For whom do I labour, and bereave my soul of good? This is also vanity, yea, it is a sore travail.[9] Two are better than one; because they have a good reward for their labour. [10] For if they fall, the one will lift up his fellow: but woe to him that is alone when he falleth; for he hath not another to help him up. [11] Again, if two lie together, then they have heat: but how can one be warm alone?[12] And if one prevail against him, two shall withstand him; and a threefold cord is not quickly broken."*

    When there is no unity one works too hard and too long will little return on your labor. This text says that two are better than one because your reward is greater. Protection is better with cooperation; if you fall the other can help you or deliver you from what you do not have the strength to do. Returning to the subject of a former chapter your Kingdom is expanded when you join forces with others. The entire chapter of 1 Corinthians 12 deals with this issue of oneness. God design the body to operate as one this is why the devil gets so much done in our communities. Prayer out of school have left our children open to the attack of the enemy. Had the body stood up things like this and others would never be. Let's hear God through Paul in 1 Corinthians 12: *[12] "For as the body is one, and hath many members, and all the members of that one body, being many, are one body: so also is Christ. [13] For by one spirit are we all baptized into one body, whether we be Jews or Gentiles, whether we be bond or free; and have been all made to drink into one spirit. [14] For the body is not one member, but many. [15] If the foot shall say, Because I am not the hand, I a not of the body; is it therefore not of the body? [16] And if the ear shall say, Because I am not the eye, I am not of the body; is it therefore not of the body? [17] If the whole body were an eye, where were the hearing? If the whole were hearing, where were the smelling? [18] But now hath God set the members every one of them in the body, as it hath pleased him. [19] And if they were all one member, where were the body? [20] But now are they many members, yet but one body. [21] And the eye cannot say unto the hand, I have no need of thee: nor again the head to the feet, I have no need of you. [22] Nay, much more those members of the body, which seem to be more feeble, are necessary: [23] And those members of the body, which we think to be less honourable, upon these we bestow more abundant honour; and our uncomely parts have more abundant comeliness. [24] For our comely parts have no need: but God hath tempered the body together, having given more abundant honour to that part which lacked. [25] That there should be no schism in the body; but that the members should have the same care one for another. [26] And whether one member suffer, all the members suffer with it; or one member be honoured, all the members rejoice with it. [27] Now ye are the body of Christ, and members in particular. [28] And God hath set some in the church, first apostles, secondarily prophets, thirdly teachers, after that miracles, then gifts of healings, helps, governments, diversities of tongues. [29] Are all apostles? are all prophets? are all teachers? are all workers of miracles? [30] Have all the gifts of healing? do all speak with tongues? do all interpret?*

³¹ But covet earnestly the best gifts: and yet shew I unto you a more excellent way."

God described us as a body fashion like that of the human body. This spiritual body like the human body was design by God for God. He places each member in his place at his will. You and I do not choose our position in the body. We are placed there by God for God. So how then can we be upset with someone for a position that he or she did not choose. I was watching a very good sermon on television this morning by Dr. Creflo Dollar, he was dealing with election. It was wonderfully and rightfully taught that God does election by his foreknowledge. He already knows what decision we will make so he sets our lives with what he knows. In this chapter God says he sets up government in the church that means he chooses who will serve where and how. So when I decide to fight the leadership I find myself fighting against God. If this is doubted listen to Romans 13: *"Let every soul be subject unto the higher powers. For there is no power but of God: the powers that be are ordained of God. ² Whosoever therefore resisteth the power, resisteth the ordinance of God: and they that resist shall receive to themselves damnation. ³ For rulers are not a terror to good works, but to the evil. Wilt thou then not be afraid of the power? do that which is good, and thou shalt have praise of the same. ⁴ For he is the minister of God to thee for good. But if thou do that which is evil, be afraid; for he beareth not the sword in vain: for he is the minister of God, a revenger to execute wrath upon him that doeth evil. ⁵ Wherefore ye must needs be subject, not only for wrath, but also for conscience sake. ⁶ For for this cause pay ye tribute also: for they are God's ministers, attending continually upon this very thing. ⁷ Render therefore to all their dues: tribute to whom tribute is due; custom to whom custom; fear to whom fear; honour to whom honour."*

God says there is no one in authority except he places them there and that we are to be subject to what he has done. He said if we obey we have nothing to fear but if we do not we will face his judgment. Authority is God's minister for good, so evil workers should be afraid.

Let's end the schism in the body and operate as one.

Next Spiritual truth: Unless God builds the house we labor in vain

Our focus cannot be on what we desire and not on the Kingdom first. We are told to seek you first the Kingdom and all of its righteousness and then the things will be added. Even in the Old Testament this principle existed and the builders of that day realized it. Ezra 3: *[2]" Then stood up Jeshua the son of Jozadak, and his brethren the priests, and Zerubbabel the son of Shealtiel, and his brethren, and builded the altar of the God of Israel, to offer burnt offerings thereon, as it is written in the Law of Moses the man of God. [3] And they set the altar upon his bases; for fear was upon them because of the people of those countries: and they offered burnt offerings thereon unto the LORD, even burnt offerings morning and evening."*

The first thing that they built was the altar of God. With all of your endeavors have you yet built an altar to your God? In other words what is the primary focus in your life is it your career or your business or your family or even your church. The most important thing should be your reference to God. God allowed us to see into his personality and declared that he is a jealous God and would have no other God before him. The first thing they did when they arrived was to build something that would allow them to give to God, they build the altar. They wanted to make sure they did it right this time. They like us had fail God and he allowed them to go into captivity. A lot of the things I have encountered were because I forgot the altar. They were fearful of the enemies that surrounded them and so should we.

God has described our enemy as a killer a thief and very destructor. When it comes to giving to God where do you stand? When we tithe we bring protection on what God has already given us. When we give God the open door into your life to bring what is needed or desired. History says there were at least four hundred years between the Old and the New Testaments. The main reasons for these years of silence by God we can find in the book of Malachi, the priest was offering sacrifices that were tainted unto God. God refuse to talk a lot to man until he found one that would offer what he desired. He found that in Christ. Paul in 2 Corinthians 8:" [9] *For ye know the grace of our Lord Jesus Christ, that, though he was rich, yet for your sakes he became poor, that ye through his poverty might be rich.* [10] *And herein I give my advice: for this is expedient for you, who have begun before, not only to do, but also to be forward a year ago.* [11] *Now therefore perform the doing of it; that as there was a readiness to will, so there may be a performance also out of that which ye have.* [12] *For if there be first a willing mind, it is accepted according to that a man hath, and not according to that he hath not.* [13] *For I mean not that other men be eased, and ye burdened:* [14] *But by an equality, that now at this time your abundance may be a supply for their want, that their abundance also may be a supply for your want: that there may be equality:* [15] *As it is written, He that had gathered much had nothing over; and he that had gathered little had no lack."*

Christ though he was rich was willing to be offered on the altar for us. He has not called us to go as far as he did by becoming poor so others could be rich. He teaches us that readiness without performance accomplishes nothing. In a future chapter I will discuss this more thoroughly. There are times when we are constantly preparing and never ever ready to perform. What you offer to God first start with you giving of yourself unto the Lord. Then you must set your mind on doing the right thing. I believe that love is a decision and not a feeling. Feelings change but you can hold on to your decision. When you read 1 Corinthians 13 there is nothing in that chapter on love that deals with a feeling. God tells us to walk by faith and not by sight.

I had the privilege for some years to sit under one of the greatest Apostles of faith Dr. Fredrick K.C. Price and in one of his teachings he teaches that when the Bible talks about walking by faith and not by sight he is talking about all of our senses. That we are not to walk by our emotions but by what it says in the word of God. Feeling being one of those emotions is not to be trusted because of its ability to constantly change. Look how many people say that they are madly in love with someone and a few days later end up in divorce court. Why did that happen because they relied on their feeling and under the pressures of life the feelings changed? I have discovered that when you change your mind your feelings follow that decision. So if one decided to love that person again their emotions will follow that decision. So Paul tells us to give according to our mind not our emotion. The reason so many people get scammed out of their money is that they move according to feelings. I have the blessing of traveling to many parts of the world to preach. I am sometimes appalled at how some people do ministry. They go somewhere in the back parts of a country or continent and find some children with swollen bellies or flies around their mouths and return with pictures or videos to use to get people to respond with their money by touching their emotions. I know some places here in America that have some kids like that but that want provoke emotion like Africa or South America.

When your mind and not your emotion is involved you cannot choose rich soil to place your seed in. It is not emotional ground that will produce for you but rich soil. Remember Jesus was rich and became poor. Only with a clear mind, will you be able to put on the altar that which will bring the most return. Let's not get all spiritual that you think your giving is for the King only. Remember David did not fight the giant for nothing there was reward. The Bible teaches that those who come to God must first believe God is and that he rewards of those who diligently seek him. Giving brings reward. Your giving is according to what you not others have. The King desires that we all get under the burden of financing the Kingdom and it not be left to a few. Sadly to say, in most churches twenty percent of the people do eighty percent of the giving. I used to be like most take my George Washington (dollar) fold it many ways and give it as though I had done God a favor.

I was in a church in Miami, Florida, when I sat on this

pew someone told me to slide over because that seat belongs to a certain lady in the church. I did not want to be out of order so I obeyed. But I had grown spiritual by that time and wanted to know what a person who owns a seat in the church gave. I was shocked when the offering came I watched closely and saw her move a roll of twenties and picked up a dime and placed it in the offering. I could not believe what I had just seen. When we discover that the altar does not only benefit God but us as well. Luke 6:38 *"Give, and it shall be given unto you; good measure, pressed down, and shaken together, and running over, shall men give into your bosom. For with the same measure that ye mete withal it shall be measured to you again."* Giving benefits the giver as well as the recipient. There is not a maybe clause in this scripture it is give and it shall be given unto you. Then with some agrarian illustrations he tells us how we shall be blessed. When trading for grain they would use large pockets on their garments or as we did large baskets. They would put the grain in and shake or pound it down and put more grain in, they would repeat this until it was running over the side. When the grain was running over the side the buyer knew he had a good deal. God is telling us to see how God will bless us if we open up our heart and our wealth to him. Remember God wants a good deal just like you. One of my favorite subjects is that of giving to your leader.

In 1 Corinthians 9: [9] *"For it is written in the Law of Moses, thou shalt not muzzle the mouth of the ox that treadeth out the corn. Doth God take care for oxen?* [10] *Or saith he it altogether for our sakes? For our sakes, no doubt, this is written: that he that ploweth should plow in hope; and that he that thresheth in hope should be partaker of his hope.* [11] *If we have sown unto you spiritual things, is it a great thing if we shall reap your carnal things?* [12] *If others be partakers of this power over you, are not we rather? Nevertheless we have not used this power; but suffer all things, lest we should hinder the gospel of Christ.* [13] *Do ye not know that they which minister about holy things live of the things of the Temple? and they which wait at the altar are partakers with the altar?* [14] *Even so hath the Lord ordained that they which preach the gospel should live of the gospel?"*

The law forbade you to put a muzzle on the mouth of an ox that grind the grain. A muzzle was something put over the mouth of an animal to keep it from stopping its work to eat. Some animal owners were so mean that they would use the ox all day long and would not allow t o eat from the grain while it worked. He said that it was written for us if one plows they should do it in hope that they too would benefit. So many Christians have adopted the theory that if you keep him humble God we will keep him poor. I will show you that is a death sentence for you. We are in this earth so there are spiritual things and carnal or flesh things. God teaches us to give some of our carnal things to the one who is giving us spiritual things. The person minister holy things live of the things of the Temple. Giving to your leader benefits you also. 3 John [2] *"Beloved, I wish above all things that thou mayest prosper and be in health, even as thy soul prospereth."*

This scripture teaches that prosperity is tied to the soul not the spirit. So we better understand salvation is in three times and three places. First we have the spirit which was saved in the past. By faith have you been saved and your sprit has he quicken, all past tense. I know we say our soul was saved but the scripture teaches that it was your spirit. He instructs us to work out our on soul salvation this is a present work. Then our bodies will be resurrected that is a future event. Each of these have an agent to carry out this work. Your spirit is like the Holy of Holy's in the Temple only the High Priest can enter and that is Christ. We are told bring our flesh under subjections. We are the one responsible for the actions of our flesh. The next component is our soul. Who is responsible for my soul, I know Christ has control of my spirit I am to work on my flesh, then who is responsible for my soul? Why is it so important, because John tells us that it is through my soul that I get prosperity and healing not my spirit?

Let's find out the answer Hebrews 13: [15] *"By him therefore let us offer the sacrifice of praise to God continually, that is, the* *fruit of our lips giving thanks to his name. *^{16}*But to do good and to communicate forget not: for with such sacrifices God is well pleased. *^{17}*Obey them that have the rule over you, and submit yourselves: for they watch for your souls, as they that must give account, that they may do it with joy, and not with grief: for that is unprofitable for you."*

Because of what God has done for us in our spirit let us praise God. Then he gives us a hidden nugget that many never discover and spend much of their lives thinking they are obeying God. Some work hard to protect what they think is the interest of the church by keeping the leader from prospering. God says that our spiritual leader is responsible for our souls. This means if you have joined a church but not the visionary you can remain in poverty and sickness. Your health and your prosperity are tied to you pastor. The more you allow the teaching of your pastor to benefit your soul you will prosper.

We all love this passage where it says the battle is not yours it is the Lords. But there is another spiritual truth we overlook in that passage. 2 Chronicles 20: ^{20}"And they rose early in the morning, and went forth into the wilderness of Tekoa: and as they went forth, Jehoshaphat stood and said, Hear me, O Judah, and ye inhabitants of Jerusalem; Believe in the LORD your God, so shall ye be established; believe his prophets, so shall ye prosper."

God gives them a spiritual truth that carries over into the New Testament. That truth is trust God to be established, but prosperity is in the prophet's mouth. If you cannot trust what comes out of your leader's mouth it is not for you to stay and battle with them you will find yourself fighting God. If you have been in the Lord for any period of time you have heard the story of Miriam and Aaron, and others who rebel against leadership and their results. The best thing to do is to find a leader you respect and can follow and become a blessing by giving your talents abilities and wealth toward the building the Kingdom. The altar is your place to bless God and to be blessed.

Chapter Nine

Monitor Your Heart Condition

When it comes to physical health people are doing what they can to prevent health problems. They are exercising more eating a proper diet taking supplements. We want to live long and healthy lives. This is a good thing, my son Jonathan is a personal trainer and sometimes have me doing all kinds of exercise. I was at a class one Saturday morning and call my wife to find out would she like to go to breakfast. She told me that Jonathan had made waffles for her and to come home he would make me some. I came back excited only to be told by son that the waffles were for mom because she needs the calories. Then he tells me you are going to have Oatmeal. Wow, my children now think that they are the parent and we are the children. Some of his workouts I never finish they are extremely hard. But I do work out with him play tennis with him because I want a strong heart. Paul tells Timothy that bodily exercise profit little. He did not say it had no profit it was just small in the general scheme of things. For you see it does not matter how you exercise eat right death is still lurking in the shadows to one day over take us. But Paul explains we are not like those that have no hope there is something on the other side of this life. I am amazed at people hard efforts for the life and no input for the next. Let's return to our text of study.

Ezra 3: [4] *"They kept also the feast of tabernacles, as it is written, and offered the daily burnt offerings by number, according to the custom, as the duty of every day required;* [5] *And afterward offered the continual burnt offering, both of the new moons, and of all the set feasts of the* Lord *that were consecrated, and of every one that willingly offered a freewill offering unto the* Lord. [6] *From the first day of the seventh month began they to offer burnt offerings unto the* Lord. *But the foundation of the temple of the* Lord *was not yet laid.* [7] *They gave money also unto the masons, and to the carpenters; and meat, and drink, and oil, unto them of Zidon, and to them of Tyre, to bring cedar trees from Lebanon to the sea of Joppa, according to the grant that they had of Cyrus king of Persia."*

No the subject is not necessarily giving but the condition of their heart that made them givers. They had a thankful heart that was expressed through their giving. If you remember in the New Testament that Jesus sat by the treasury and watch the givers. You can always tell when God has done a work in the heart of a believer because of their giving. Jesus notices that the highly religious people hearts had not been changed. But this highly devoted widow's heart had surely been changed. Another way you know that your heart is healed is how you respond to sin.

For the sake of this teaching I will give the time I knew that God had healed my sin sick heart. I was in Bible College and we had a dinner one night in which I invited one of my old girl friends. We had a wonderful time at the dinner. I returned her to her home and she invited me in. I told her thanks but no thanks got in my car and left. This was the night that I realized what God had done in me. Just a few weeks prior to this night I would not have had the strength to walk away and not go in. Praise God! Your heart change has a lot to do with your obedience. We had a united worship service in our city. I was seated in the pulpit of one of those churches, a young teenager sitting behind me in the choir leaned forward and asked did I remember her and I said I did not. She then re minded me that I once dated her mother. I then remember, she asked after the service could she be given a ride home I agreed. When we arrived at her home she said you should come in and say hello to mom. I said I believe I will, at that moment I heard God as though he were on the loudest PA available tell me to get back in that car. I apologized to the young girl told her to tell her mom hello for me and I left.

Another heart check can come when you have been offended. God gave me something years ago that has been with me through these many years of ministry. It was this, "anything you take personally I want but if you do not I will. He told me that you are not all that for people to come against you. They come against you because of the oil of anointing upon you and the words I put in your mouth. It is not you that they are rejecting but me, so let me handle it." Listen to this God said "vengeance is not wrong it is just mine". I have learned to be afraid for the people that come against me rather than to be upset because they did. When you know God's love and wants to use you, then you want worry when others try to stop you with their words or actions.

Paul tells us "that all things work together for those who love God and that are called according to his purpose". Notice we are human and do not like the things said are done against us. So what they do against is not good but will eventually work out for good. If I have shared this before remember I am a senior and we actually do have those moments. I was lied on when I left Fort Wayne Indiana to move to Tampa Florida My church had reached an all time high in attendance. I was leaving and people could not figure it out. When people cannot figure a thing out they will create something that make sense to them. It was put out that I was dealing drugs and moving to get closer to my source. The person who started the lie would need my help later. I know that the offense hurt my heart but not my mission I still moved and God still moves in my life. If you do not deal with offense the writer of Hebrews says that a root of bitterness can spring up. I can go on and on about the things of the heart but you get the picture if your heart has been strengthen by exercising spiritual truths in your life you know it and if not you know that as well and need to submit that part of your life to God.

The next spiritual truth: Success can only come when purpose is discovered

Ezra 3:8 *[8"] Now in the second year of their coming unto the house of God at Jerusalem, in the second month, began Zerubbabel the son of Shealtiel, and Jeshua the son of Jozadak, and the remnant of their brethren the priests and the Levites, and all they that were come out of the captivity unto Jerusalem; and appointed the Levites, from twenty years old and upward, to set forward the work of the house of the* LORD. *⁹ Then stood Jeshua with his sons and his brethren, Kadmiel and his sons, the sons of Judah, together, to set forward the workmen in the house of God: the sons of Henadad, with their sons and their brethren the Levites".*

One of the greatest teachers of our time on this subject is Dr. Myles Monroe, I call him Mr. Purpose. I do advise you to get any of his books on purpose and the Kingdom. I have never read one of his books and did not get inspired. If you have not discovered purpose you will misuse and abuse your life. I did for years, I did not know my purpose so I abused my life and those that were tied to my life. When I was a young man one of the phrases of the day was that we were looking for ourselves. Most of us never discovered ourselves because we were looking in the wrong place. One of the things Dr. Monroe teaches is that if you want to know purpose you must read the manual. You do not go to Chevy to have your Ford worked on. You go to the origin of the thing. Everything that God made must stay attached to the place God made it to live. For example a fish must stay in the water and plants and trees in the ground. When God made man he attached him to himself. So man must stay close to God to develop and grow.

We like these tribes try to do our own thing without God. We leave God out until there is a tragedy and then we want him involved. We have had some terrible things to happen to our children in the place we thought was safe. In school children have to run for their lives from crazed shooters. We told God that he was not welcome on our campuses he could not be studied or worshiped there. Yet when there is a problem we ask where was God. I read what is to be a true story of a young lady that was going out for a night of fun, her mother did not want her to go but she insisted. Her mother being a believer told her make certain she takes the Lord with her. She told her mom that the car would be full and if Jesus wanted to go he must ride in the trunk. That night she had a terrible accident and everyone in the car was killed, but in the trunk was a crate of eggs and not one was broken. The trunk was where she said Jesus could ride.

After one of the most deadly shooting on a school grounds in US history a reporter ask a female evangelist where was God in all of this. The Evangelist reminded her that we had excused Jesus from our schools and that he being a gentleman responded to our request. God had given Israel specific instructions on how to live and work and everything he told them surrounded their worship and devotion to their God. But they like us got caught up in their environment wanting to be like and accepted by those around them and forgot their purpose. You must know by now that you were not created just to go to work pick up a paycheck at the end of the pay period and then go do it all over again. Paul said if only in this life we have Christ we are men most miserable. You have a purpose and the purpose must be discovered for you to have a full life.

Proverbs tells us to trust God and not to lean on our own understanding, in all your ways acknowledge him and he would direct our path. You cannot discover your purpose without the help of God the designer. Their rejection of God had caused them to be thrust from the land God had given them and to meet the hardship of slavery. God ask Saul who became Paul a question. Why do you keep kicking against the pricks? Paul being raised in that time knew what God was talking about. Oxen were used to plow fields and to carry heavy burdens and sometime they would lose focus on purpose and stop are get off track and driver would have to prick them with a pointed stick to get them to go in the direction the driver had in mind. Paul like some of us was very religious and doing what he thought was the will of God. My younger sister Brenda was not like me she was compliant and tried to please our parents. She was very smart and graduated from college, met and married one of the greatest men God made. Went to church but not quite sure of her relationship with God or his purpose for her. She and her husband came to visit me and we had a movie night, the movie we played was a thief in the night. The movie had a great effect on her life and more than that she saw the life of the worst brother she had changed. When she returned to Miami she called me and said these words "Jr. I want whatever it is that you have." She and her wonderful husband are both preachers of the Gospel of Jesus Christ.

I wished time would permit me to tell the stories of multiplied thousands of people who God allowed me to minister to that are now operating in their purpose. That is another part of this discovery that I need to mention, that God will use others to help direct you into your destiny. I was in a night club one night and having what I thought was a good time. My good time was interrupted by a man that had quite too much to drink. He came over to my table and said you do not belong in here you are a preacher. I must confess I wanted to hurt him badly not just because of what he said but because I knew that what he said was true. Also in a club a man said to me you do not go to church because of hypocrites? I told him that he was right. He said a hypocrite is a low man isn't he? I said yes. Then he spoke these words "it takes a lower man to hide behind him." I got the message. God can and will use anyone he pleases to help you get to purpose.

So many people who are happy doing the work of the Lord are there not because God spoke directly but because he spoke through another servant and their spirit understood that God was using them. God even used the king of a heathen nation to put Israel back on purpose. Nehemiah and Ezra received help from a foreign king. I remember two young ladies that are still working with me after twenty plus years that I told that God would use. Both showed great fear on their face when they were told. Their names are Millicent Stephenson and Darlene Lundy they are now both powerful women of God.

This is why it is so important you do not have a leader you just tolerate and not celebrate. Remember the thirteen chapter of Hebrews states we could lead an unprofitable life by disobeying our leaders. God will not take any of your excuses about why you are disobedient. I want to remind you again about the scripture train up a child in the way it should go and it want depart. This scripture is dealing with purpose, it said train the way it should go. This again is talking about destiny and purpose. If you help them find the way they can remain on it, but sometimes we need to help them find it. That is why mentoring books like this and others are so important it helps us help others. Please teach your ward to listen for the voice of God directly and through others.

The next spiritual truth: Secure growth comes from a solid foundation

Ezra 3: *[10] "And when the builders laid the foundation of the temple of the Lord, they set the priests in their apparel with trumpets, and the Levites the sons of Asaph with cymbals, to praise the Lord, after the ordinance of David king of Israel. [11] And they sang together by course in praising and giving thanks unto the Lord; because he is good, for his mercy endureth for ever toward Israel. And all the people shouted with a great shout, when they praised the Lord, because the foundation of the house of the Lord was laid."*

I built a large church building in Fort Wayne Indiana. I like most get excited with building something new. I had drawn so many plans until I came up with this one. They were given to the architect to draw to scale and to get approval. Now the building process began. I was onsite many times a day to see the progress only to be disappointed. They to me were moving so slow. I ask what was going on we are paying you and it does not seem like nothing is happening. The builder told me that a lot of things were happening that was not visible yet. He said this is the slowest part of the process. The foundation was being built. The work of the foundation was tedious and long but very necessary. I was told the foundation size and weight will determine the height and weight of the rest of the building. When I was in Bible College many wanted me to start doing more. Some wanted me to travel and tell my testimony of the delivering power of God. I had live a life involved in drugs prostitution and the occult. But I refuse because I wanted a sound foundation under me first. Listen to Paul advice to Timothy 3: [6] *"Not a novice, lest being lifted up with pride he fall into the condemnation of the devil.* [7] *Moreover he must have a good report of them which are without; lest he fall into reproach and the snare of the devil.* If the foundation is not solid the enemy will be able to knock you off course. Pride is a hard thing to keep out of your when you are mature and impossible when you are young. So the two things that must be present in this scripture are impossible without a strong foundation. One is to keep pride away and two is to have a good report from without. Without having a strong foundation, both of these are impossibilities. I will deal with this subject later but for now I will say people are more concern about their image than they are about their character. Image is what others think of you and character is who you really are.

How will I know my foundation is weak? Look for yourself in this next passage of scriptures. 1 Timothy 3: [14] *"For all the law is fulfilled in one word, even in this; Thou shalt love thy neighbour as thyself.* [15] *But if ye bite and devour one another, take heed that ye be not consumed one of another.* [16] *This I say then, Walk in the spirit, and ye shall not fulfill the lust of the flesh.* [17] *For the flesh lusteth against the spirit, and the spirit against the flesh: and these are contrary the one to the other: so that ye cannot do the things that ye would.* [18] *But if ye be led of the spirit, ye are not under the law.* [19] *Now the works of the flesh are manifest, which are these; Adultery, fornication, uncleanness, lasciviousness.* [20] *Idolatry, witchcraft, hatred, variance, emulations, wrath, strife, seditions, heresies* [21] *Envyings, murders, drunkenness, revellings, and such like: of the which I tell you before, as I have also told you in time past, that they which do such things shall not inherit the Kingdom of God."*

The whole basis if the Kingdom walk is summed up in the word love. Love in the context of the Kingdom is to desire the best for others. The opposite of this kind of love is not hatred but is to be self center. If you look at the list in the preceding scripture they all focus on you the individual. Witchcraft is even listed as a work of the flesh, for it is only a desire to have power over others. Lust a desire to have your needs met not caring about the other. Husbands and wives could have this selfishness even in their marriage. Your ministry or career is about to fall sooner or later if these things exist in your life. In my past I have committed adultery I was not concern with what would happen to the woman I was laying with nor the feeling and emotion of her husband. When you cause strife and division you do not care about the hurt you bring. When you gossip you are not concern about the hurt you bring to neither the person you are talking about nor the one you are talking to. All these things show that your foundation is weak and eventually your walls will come tumbling down.

Now I have discovered what a weak wall looks like what does a strong wall look like? *Galatians 3:* [22] *"But the fruit of the spirit is love, joy, peace, longsuffering, gentleness, goodness, faith,* [23] *Meekness, temperance: against such there is no law.* [24] *And they that are Christ's have crucified the flesh with the affections and lusts.* [25] *If we live in the spirit, let us also walk in the spirit.* [26] *Let us not be desirous of vain glory, provoking one another, envying one another."*

Remember that our foundation is Christ. 1 *Corinthians 3:* [11] *"For other foundation can no man lay than that is laid, which is Jesus Christ."*

You can only build when there is a foundation to build on, and in the Christian's it is Christ. So in order to build you must use the same materials, If we are building a brick house we cannot in the middle decide to use wood. If the foundation was built for a steel building you cannot decide to use brick. Paul said you cannot build except on that which has been laid and that is Christ. Christ is many things but one he is love and the father is a spirit. So your building must be made out of these two materials. Paul tells us the fruit of the spirit so what you are building must come out of the spirit or it is a waste of time. In this group of scriptures the light is off of us and on what the spirit has produced in our lives. If you have allowed him to work his work through you it will be impossible for what you are building to come down.

The people of Ezra's day began to praising God because of the foundation. How many times have you praise God because you now have the ability to love the unlovable, to be humble because you have joy and peace your faith is strong. Most of what we rejoice about are things we can see. Most of the foundational work done in you; only you can see and might never be recognized by others. You and I need a strong foundation to build what God has placed in our hearts. So spend more time on your foundation than anything else.

Examine this truth: You must be willing to change: Ezra 3: *[12]" But many of the priests and Levites and chief of the fathers, who were ancient men, that had seen the first house, when the foundation of this house was laid before their eyes, wept with a loud voice; and many shouted aloud for joy: [13] So that the people could not discern the noise of the shout of joy from the noise of the weeping of the people: for the people shouted with a loud shout, and the noise was heard afar off."*

I believe that one of the most difficult things for man to do is change because we are creatures of habit. I have heard this for years and believe it. The enemy of the new move of God is the old move of God. When I started ministry in the 1970's it seems ancient now. All the churches in my community were very orthodox in their styles. Now if you were from the outside of my community and visited those churches you would say I was crazy. But to describe the worship, it was very high powered and the preaching was dynamic in its presentation but low in its content. Sunday school is where you were taught the Bible because the books were purchase from companies outside of the community. The Sunday school books were systematic in its presentation so if you came to Sunday school you would be taught the scripture. But the down side of that was the same people who led in the church gave you their own swing on the teaching.

Preaching in my community as I personally observed came from the times when men in my community were uneducated and relied heavily on the outside community for its learning. So the pastor would take one verse or maybe two or three and expound on them. You had a lot of fillers to cover up the lack of content. I am not knocking this style of preaching it is my culture and I love my culture. I am mentioning this to show mans hatred of change. Some pastors are more educated and still use this style without increasing content. I to use this style occasionally because it feels good and I like it and it is my culture but I add content. I was told by my pastor from the neighborhood, that I would not make it as a pastor. It hurt my heart so much that even now I can visualize the place and content of that conversation. The reason he told me that I would not make it was not because he thought I could not do it. It was because I did not adapt the style of preaching that had been in our community for years. I was not disrespectful in my reply but told him to keep doing it your way and I will do what God was leading me to do and we will see.

When you are in a community where you are different you stick out like my mother use to say a sore thumb. We built a large size church in that community I will share some of the technique I use, not for you to utilize all of them some were for that season. I had to be willing to make a change, and listen, and learn to deal with the ridicule of the change. We were reluctantly voted pastor of the year in 1987 along with another pastor something that had never happen before but they just could not just celebrate change alone. Yet I was now pastor of the year and they had a banquet in my honor and had my pastor as the speaker.

God is something else; I will prepare a table before you in the presence of your enemies. The Lord permitted me to honor my pastor and make him a Bishop in 1999. These things took place because I was able to push pass my fears and change. We were deemed the church that had the people no one else wanted. We went to the streets the bars, homes where ever there were people we went. We won prostituted to the Lord disciple them and put them back on the corner to win other prostitutes. We went to our police and got badges for them to have so if there was a bust they would not be arrested. I would give men money to buy the prostitute; we would actually pay her for her time but not her service and witness to her. We purchase a transitional house to house these ladies in. We help them go to school or find jobs. So many were saved that a contract was placed on my head, the police actually caught the men and show me the contract. We had young people doing Christian rap and dance. In our colleges, the kids in frats and sororities did step we allowed them to step in the church. We would some time celebrate at the end of the service with a line dance called the electric slide, a staple in our community. I mention these things and believe me there were many more to show you the power of change. I have discovered and have adapted to the fact that a lot of the things I did back then will not work today and I have to change. If I do not change I am the pastors that were in place when I came alone but just a different time. If you are not utilizing technology in you worship experiences you have not been aware that change has come again. I now do a mid-week service on a telephone line connected to my computer, and right now have members in ten states and two countries in my class.

    If you will look at the preceding passage you will see that the new Temple is now built and it is celebration time. But memories have dampened the celebration of some. There were lots of jubilant expressions taking place over the finished work of a few slaves that had been set free. When you work hard it is ok to play hard or to give God thanks for his aid in the accomplishment of your project. But as it is in many endeavors in life many will not able to celebrate with you. The Bible tells us that while this worship was going on there were different sounds going at the same time. There were people crying because they were old enough to remember the first Temple. I can't say this of this people but I will of others, some cannot celebrate with you because secretly they were hoping you would fail. Memories make change hard, for many people live in the past and cannot leave to embrace change.

Kingship Examination

What is the blue print of the King?

1. His thoughts

2. His plans

3. The word of God

4. His goals

Success is reach when God, His favor, His vision, and timing is in place

1. True

2. False

One of the greatest components of success is Synergy (working together) Ecclesiastes 4:9

1. True

2. False

Division is a work of the enemy

1. True

2. False

Success is accomplished by honoring the Kings in your life Ezra 3:2-3

1. True

2. False

Kings love the Altar Ezra 3:2-3

1. True

2. False

Giving is a priority in success 1 Corinthians 9:9-14

1. True

2. False

Giving to my leader is a sign of maturity Hebrews 13:15-17

1. True

2. False

I can measure my growth through my giving (Jesus sat by the giving)

1. True

2. False

Purpose must be known to reach success

1. True

2. False

More time on the foundation is need more than anywhere else (prayer, love, giving, Bible study, church attendance, service, witnessing

1. True

2. False

King to do list

- Study five chapters in your Bible
- Ask God for a vision favor and timing
- Practice working in harmony with others
- Be a peacemaker and do not be divisive
- Honor God and your leader
- Develop a prayer life and go to the altar for repentance when needed
- Start tithing and giving (tithe is ten percent of your income and giving starts after you have paid your tithe)
- Give special offerings to your leader for your benefit
- Chart your giving and you see how you are growing spiritually
- Pray and depend on your leader to guide you into purpose
- Spend most of your time on your foundation, Loving God and man, Studying the word, prayer, character building, giving, church attendance, witnessing

Chapter Ten

Evil and your destiny

I was in the shower reflecting on a decision I made with the influence of another person that did not do what they said they would. I was thinking that this person could have been used to altar my destiny or get me away from it. It was there that God spoke to my heart and said that he has often used evil things and people to get his people to their destiny. I said wow! I have read the scripture about God's emotion toward me and he said he had no evil thoughts. Let's look at it now.

Jeremiah 29: ¹⁰ For thus saith the LORD, *That after seventy years be accomplished at Babylon I will visit you, and perform my good word toward you, in causing you to return to this place. ¹¹ For I know the thoughts that I think toward you, saith the* LORD, *thoughts of peace, and not of evil, to give you an expected end".*

Judah, found themselves in an evil situation that God permitted. He even told them how long they would be there seventy years. Time is relative to the situation he was here dealing with a nation and more time was needed. When you find yourself in a difficult place it is easy to accuse God of not loving you are that he is in plotting against you. God tells them he is going to use the enemy for seventy years against them and the he said I know my thought s are not evil against you. The purpose of evil is to destroy you that you never rise again yet going in God tells them they are coming out. God's thoughts are not evil yet he uses evil to point you toward destiny. Remember the devil comes to kill steal and destroy. God is trying to get you somewhere and he uses evil and sometimes evil people to get you there.

I love what Paul tells us in Romans 8: *²⁷ And he that searcheth the hearts knoweth what is the mind of the spirit, because he maketh intercession for the saints according to the will of God. ²⁸ And we know that all things work together for good to them that love God, to them who are the called according to his purpose".*

Most of us know and love verse twenty-eight but there is a preceding verse. God searches the heart and knows the mind of the spirit. Because of this he prays that I stay on destiny. This destiny must line up with the will of God. So sometimes adverse situations make you remember how far off track you are. Remember this text does not say that all things are good but they in the end will work out for good for those who love God and called according to his purpose. God show me many people that evil situations or people helped someone to arrive at their destiny let's look at a few.

Genesis 13:⁵ And Lot also, which went with Abram, had flocks, and herds, and tents. ⁶ And the land was not able to bear them, that they might dwell together: for their substance was great, so that they could not dwell together. ⁷ And there was a strife between the herdmen of Abram's cattle and the herdmen of Lot's cattle: and the Canaanite and the Perizzite dwelled then in the land. ⁸ And Abram said unto Lot, Let there be no strife, I pray thee, between me and thee, and between my herdmen and thy herdmen; for we be brethren. ⁹ Is not the whole land before thee? separate thyself, I pray thee, from me: if thou wilt take the left hand, then I will go to the right; or if thou depart to the right hand, then I will go to the left. ¹⁰ And Lot lifted up his eyes, and beheld all the plain of Jordan, that it was well watered every where, before the LORD *destroyed Sodom and Gomorrah, even as the garden of the* LORD, *like the land of Egypt, as thou comest unto Zoar".*

I have found times when the worst things you can do is work with family which should be the easiest. Because Lot was with Abraham he was blessed too, that is another story. Some of our blessings like our curses come from attachments. There was a family argument that could not be settled with words only distance. I heard Dr Price say on many occasion if I find out that you are a liar I will love you from a distance. That is good preaching. We try to hold on to some people and give them a better opportunity to destroy you when you arrive at your destiny. It is sometimes best to let them go before they can do more damage.

Wars develop out of lust. I know some of you are thinking that was his herdsmen not him. In Business College we had to study fail businesses and those that went through transition back to success. One was a company that bought failed golf courses and rebuilt them. I was shocked at one of their practices. Every time they purchase a golf course the first thing they did was to fire the leadership of that club. Their theory was that a place rise and falls on leadership and if this place was going to be successful with them it already would be. It was not just Lot's herdsmen it was Lot he lack something in his leadership one was Agape Love. The opposite of Agape love is not hatred but to be self center. Notice the action of Lot when given an opportunity to choose. He chose he thought was the best land, selfish. He had no regard for his uncle who had put him in the success he now enjoys.

But now let's examine what happens to Abraham next. Genesis 13: *[14] And the LORD said unto Abram, after that Lot was separated from him, Lift up now thine eyes, and look from the place where thou art northward, and southward, and eastward, and westward: [15] For all the land which thou seest, to thee will I give it, and to thy seed for ever. [16] And I will make thy seed as the dust of the earth: so that if a man can number the dust of the earth, then shall thy seed also be numbered. [17] Arise, walk through the land in the length of it and in the breadth of it; for I will give it unto thee.*

It is amazing but there are some people in your presence that is keeping you from seeing your destiny. They must be removed, so you can even hear the voice of God. It was only after he had been separate from Lot because of an evil situation that God shows him his destiny. God not only show him his destiny but told him how to possess it. That evil person or condition will not destroy you but it is temporary. You will get to the other side of it and if you do it was a God thing and not an evil thing.

One of my favorite persons of the Bible is that of Joseph. Joseph like many of us was a dreamer. One thing that I as dreamer found out is the moment God gives me one I want to tell someone about it. The second thing I found out is that you cannot tell everyone. Sadly to say there is spiritual abortionist all around us waiting to destroy your dream in its infancy. Joseph made the mistake of sharing his dream with his brothers and his father. I learn something's from Joseph's experience one is brothers cannot handle your throne being exalted if it will exceed theirs. Fathers have been dreamers and you can share because the thought process is different. He may not understand your dream but because of past experience will ponder it. Because he shared his dream his brothers conspired against him. When one person dislikes you or your dream they will employ others to feel the same way thus a conspiracy. They started by removing this coat that his father had given him. The boys knew that this coat represented Joseph's destiny to be king over the family so they took it from him. There are some of you that some things or some person job career home or auto have been taken from you.

Although it was an evil act maybe God permitted it to happen, remember that if it is God there will be an exit door. Joseph's destiny was bigger than what he or his father had envisioned. The coat that Joseph would eventually get would give him authority over more than the one he had on. Listen to this and I hope it changes your destiny; you cannot wear two coats one must be removed to put on the other. Some of the evil acts can be used to enlarge your territory. Joseph's destiny would lead him to be the leader over a nation that would give him authority over the family as well. Quit crying over your lost and look for the next coat. I know right now it seems like you are in Hell because of something that has taken place in your life. But I assure you it is only a temporary event that will propel you to your throne. I f God is in it there is a door of exit look for it and choose it when it arrives. Deuteronomy

30:19 I call heaven and earth to record this day against you, that I have set before you **life** and death, blessing and cursing: therefore **choose life**, that both thou and thy seed may live.

Life is filled with choices, that is why God tells us in all your ways acknowledge him and he will direct your path of your choices. The evil in Joseph's life transcended his home land. Listen some places you are now had it not been for an evil event you would not be there. Some person left you broke your heart but now you have either found someone better or have peace that you are alone not lonely alone. There may be future events that cause you to change location. I have just changed locations and because of it discovered my purpose for today. I have been doing the same thing in the Kingdom for years and now God has change my assignment and used someone who made promises and did not fulfill them because my wife and I did not allow them to run our lives. Say with me change is good no matter how it comes. I should have reminded you of the dry pit he was placed in before been sold by his brothers to a hard life of slavery.

We as black Americans were brought over here in chains and deplorable conditions by evil men but do not forget we were first sold by our brothers. Just like the coat you have to leave to get the new ones we must leave those places and people and condition to enter the throne. The hole Joseph's was placed in was deep enough to keep and dry. Some of you feel right now that you are in a deep hole and it is dry no water. Water in the scripture is sometimes used to describe the spirit. There are times when we are in a place where we cannot seem to get out the hole is not the only worry it seems as though God does not care you cannot feel or experience is presence. Joseph was in a whole with no signs of life. He is sold to a owner in Egypt and he likes his job and can do it well. He is falsely accused and thrown in prison because as a king he had authority over his flesh. He is given favor even in prison. Some of you are in a prison like circumstance even as you are reading this book but somehow, some way, God seems to always come through for you. That is called favor. He helps two men see their destiny and ask one to remember him, to which he was forgotten. Finally it is time he is brought to the throne. When it is your time nothing will be able to stop you but you must wait. What was Joseph's attitude concerning those who place him in those deplorable situations?

Genesis 50: [15] And when Joseph's brethren saw that their father was dead, they said, Joseph will peradventure hate us, and will certainly requite us all the evil which we did unto him. [16] And they sent a messenger unto Joseph, saying, Thy father did command before he died, saying. [17] So shall ye say unto Joseph, Forgive, I pray thee now, the trespass of thy brethren, and their sin; for they did unto thee evil: and now, we pray thee, forgive the trespass of the servants of the God of thy father. And Joseph wept when they spake unto him. [18] And his brethren also went and fell down before his face; and they said, Behold, we be thy servants. [19] And Joseph said unto them, Fear not: for am I in the place of God? [20] But as for you, ye thought evil against me; but God meant it unto good, to bring to pass, as it is this day, to save much people alive. [21] Now therefore fear ye not: I will nourish you, and your little ones. And he comforted them, and spake kindly unto them".

The tables are turned Joseph's is no longer that little boy but a grown man and the leader of a powerful African nation. His father is dead and would no longer have in influence on his decisions. His brothers of very much aware of his authority, and there new circumstance. They send a message to their brother sharing their father's wishes. They stated their guilt and that what was done to him was evil and they also wanted his forgiveness. Notice the maturity and spiritual understanding in Joseph's reply. Joseph understood that what they did to him was put him on the right course to fulfill his destiny. He named the throne in Egypt the place of God. He understood that the place he was now in was orchestrated by God himself even using the evil of his on brothers. So he assured them that they had nothing to fear, he allowed them to see their own guilt in their action but that

God used their evil decision to get him to the throne. He then said something that help shape my life, he said I will nourish you. Wow! Man and woman of God if when you arrive at your throne if your heart have not been changed so you can forgive and help the ones that hurt you along the way you are not ready for the throne. Yes you heard me right that man that divorced you and left you to raise all those children by yourself, that woman that ran off with your best friend and the banker that took your house and car the boss that fired you on Christmas day. You see what I mean you must forgive and be ready to aid them if they would need it. I shared this with you early in the book that God said vengeance is not wrong but belong to him. You can see why it might be a destiny move.

The Pharaoh in your life could have been employed by God to get you to the throne of your destiny. Romans 9:17 For the scripture saith unto Pharaoh, *Even for this same purpose ha ve I raised thee up, that I might shew my power in thee, and that my name might be declared throughout all the earth'.*

Kingship Examination

God uses evil people and circumstances to help us reach destiny

1. True

2. False

God has evil thoughts about us Jeremiah 29:11

1. True

2. False

According to Romans 8:28 things are always good

1. True

2. False

Separating from others is sometimes God's will Genesis 13:7-8

1. True

2. False

Others sometimes block your view of destiny Genesis 13:15-17

1. True

2. False

So we should hate those who did us evil

1. True

2. False

King to do List

- Look at the times when evil situations brought **you to good things**

- **Remind yourself God is not thinking evil about me**

- **Know that even the bad things will work out because you love God and his purpose**

- **There maybe people you will have to leave to get to your destiny**

- **See if someone is keeping you from the blessings of God**

- **Do not hate the evil purpose but discover their purpose for helping you reach your destiny**

Chapter Eleven
Closing the Door of Offense

I have been in the ministry since 1976, and have had to deal with all kinds of people and so will you. It is important that we understand right from the beginning that no matter how good you are you will not be able to please everyone. Some people that you are close to right now will not be with you later in life. I was in a seminar and the teacher was Bishop Robert Vinson, a powerful man of God. He taught, "With every level we have new friends". In most cases, you do not have the same friends you had in kindergarten, elementary school, high school or even college. There are always exceptions to this rule. In most cases as you ascend to your place of ruler ship you lose and gain new friends along the way. Some people cannot go with you even though you want them to. One of the greatest tragedies of our time was a great football player who tried his best to take his old friends with him. Charged for murder and currently incarcerated for what he did. Another is trying to put his life back together after serving time in prison for trying to lift his friends from the neighborhood. It is also certain that you will get offended along the way. So how does a king deal with offense?

Hebrews 12: [15] *"Looking diligently lest any man fail of the grace of God; lest any root of bitterness springing up trouble you, and thereby many be defiled;"*

If I know the purpose behind a thing, then I know how to use or avoid being hurt by it. The ultimate goal of the enemy when he brings me offense is to get me to fall from God's grace. Wow, that put a new perspective on offense. It is more than a person trying to get me upset; it is an assault on the grace of God in my life. Becoming bitter for any reason hurts you probably more than it hurts the one you are angry with. The grace of God in your life surely outweighs in value holding something against the person who offended you.

Offense comes from the Greek word skandalon, which means bait stick- something used to catch and trap small animals and birds. I am already mad because of the adjective used in this definition, small. To allow ourselves to be trapped by offense shows the level of our growth, I will speak to this in a moment. This Greek word is where we get the word scandal. Scandal is where wrong action motivated by wrong motives will get you trapped. Therefore, offense is a trap for small kings. Let us repeat that offense is a trap for kings.

Offense is a sign of immaturity

Remember it is to catch small things; you are too small to see what the outcome will be. *James 1:* ¹⁴ *"But every man is tempted, when he is drawn away of his own lust, and enticed.* ¹⁵ *Then when lust hath conceived, it bringeth forth sin: and sin, when it is finished, bringeth forth death".*

A king, like an attorney should never deal with a subject that the answer is not already known. We should know the outcome in any matter because you know your God. In the past, I learned to be more upset for the person bringing the offense than for me receiving it. Because I already know the answer, God said vengeance is mine I will repay. The offense will not hurt me as much as living without the grace of God. I share this, not for my benefit but to show you the importance of this teaching. A young woman in my church met a young man and wanted to marry him. I knew that it would not work even though this man was a minister. I begged her not to do it she said to me that I know you are right but I still want to do it. Remember that it is the duty of the watchman to warn not enforce. I told her what God said to me about the matter that she would be home in six months. God must know a few things because the pastor had the marriage annulled telling his congregants that he was in lust not love and she returned home in six months still angry with me and not speaking. There was another woman in my church who was healed of cancer in my ministry and her mother of a stroke. She encouraged the young woman to ignore Bishop and do what she wanted. One day I asked her was she not afraid to challenge what God had given me. Her answer was very sharp and to the point. She said not only did I do it I would do it again. I was terrified for her and with good reason within, I believe a month the cancer was back and she was dead. You see when you have understanding you do not have time to be offended.

Another woman in my first church left the church and began spreading lies on me. She lost her mind, and was placed in a mental institution, and because of danger to herself and others was placed in a padded room and placed in a straight jacket. She was not speaking with much intelligence but they kept hearing her call out my name. I was asked to come and see her to which I replied in the affirmative. When I arrived, she was on the floor crouched in a corner. I spoke to her by name, she looked up at me and asked me to forgive her I said I would and instantly her mind returned. I moved later from the city but even when she died, she had requested that I do her home going service. You see her life could have had a tragic end, if I could not see the trap that was set. My Bishop used to tell me something that did not seem to make a lot of sense. He would say you are "too big to be little." When you are trapped by offense, it shows your immaturity. James teaches that the focus is on something you want or is lusting for if you have no personal agenda then you cannot be trapped.

Offense can be tied to your tradition or mindset

The Latin word offedere- means to strike against, so when you are offended someone has striked out at something you trust or believe in. Let us look at an example of that in the life and teaching of Jesus.

John 6: [49] *"Your fathers did eat manna in the wilderness, and are dead. ⁵⁰ This is the bread which cometh down from heaven, that a man may eat thereof, and not die. ⁵¹ I am the living bread which came down from heaven: if any man eat of this bread, he shall live for ever: and the bread that I will give is my flesh, which I will give for the life of the world. ⁵² The Jews therefore strove among themselves, saying, How can this man give us his flesh to eat? ⁵³ Then Jesus said unto them, Verily, verily, I say unto you, Except ye eat the flesh of the Son of man, and drink his blood, ye have no life in you. ⁵⁴ Whoso eateth my flesh, and drinketh my blood, hath eternal life; and I will raise him up at the last day. ⁵⁵ For my flesh is meat indeed, and my blood is drink indeed. ⁵⁶ He that eateth my flesh, and drinketh my blood, dwelleth in me, and I in him. ⁵⁷ As the living Father hath sent me, and I live by the Father: so he that eateth me, even he shall live by me. ⁵⁸ This is that bread which came down from heaven: not as your fathers did eat manna, and are dead: he that eateth of this bread shall live for ever. ⁵⁹ These things said he in the synagogue, as he taught in Capernaum. ⁶⁰ Many therefore of his disciples, when they had heard this, said, This is an hard saying; who can hear it? ⁶¹ When Jesus knew in himself that his disciples murmured at it, he said unto them, Doth this offend you?"*

Jesus in verse sixty-one asked his disciples did his statement offend them. In verse sixty-two he showed them as long as you have tradition that caused offense will continually be offended. John 6: ⁶²"What and if ye shall see the Son of man ascend up where he was before?"

Under Jewish law they were aware of the penalty of eating anything with its blood and Jesus now seem to be challenging their tradition. 1 Samuel 14:34 "And Saul said, Disperse yourselves among the people, and say unto them, Bring me hither every man his ox, and every man his sheep, and slay them here, and eat; and sin **not** against the Lord in **eating** with the **blood**. And all the people brought every man his ox with him that night, and slew them there."

There were things in my tradition that kept me from growing in the things of God. God tried to take me to the next level and I was holding on to tradition. One of the men

I fore mentioned was a great influence in my life, later in my life he told me that I was one in his. I was raised in the same denomination, as he and he at one time was my pastor. Our denomination fought some things as much as they preached the gospel. They fought the work of the Holy Spirit in this season. He told me after I was able to fight my way through my tradition to receive the Holy Spirit's work in my life. He said God called him to do what I was doing, to lay hands on the sick and that they would recover. He said he was not going to fight any longer but would travel to my next destination with me to conduct healing services. I told him that I was going to Jamaica; he said he was going with me I was so excited. Sadly, to say he did not make it, I went to his home going service and left there for Jamaica. An old preacher used to tell us that sin will take you farther than you want to go and keep you longer than you want to stay and cost you more than you could ever pay.

Sin is disobedience. He waited too late and that was only to fulfilled tradition. These people were offended by Jesus teaching and could not arrive to the level of growth needed to move forward. I want you to notice that Jesus was not a small person concerned with his personal agenda. He pointed to the problem they would have because of the offense he did not take it personally. He told them they would not be able to receive deeper teaching if this offended them. What is in your life that has become your sacred cow that God cannot give you more revelation because it would strike out at what you already believe? Small people wrap themselves around a teaching while Kings wrap themselves around the teacher. So many people join a church and not a visionary. Selah

Offended people blame others but Jesus said it is your response that matters

Matthew 13:[20] "But he that received the seed into stony places, the same is he that heareth the word, and anon with joy receiveth it; [21] Yet hath he not root in himself, but dureth for a while: for when tribulation or persecution ariseth because of the word, by and by he

is offended".

There are people that are still angry with others who are no longer on the earth. There are people who do not go to church because of offense. Dr. E.V. Hill was a powerful man of God. He tells the story of a town where he preached. He caught a cab, the driver asked was he preaching at a certain church, and he said yesssss, the way he could only drag yes out. The driver told him that he did not go to church and gave him the reason. He said that the same people that he picked up on Sunday for church, he carries to the club on Saturday. Therefore, their actions had offended him. Dr. Hill in away only he could do told him a story. He said I am staying in the hotel here in the city and tomorrow a young man will come to pick my shirts up to carry them to the laundry. He asked the driver, should I give the boy my dirty shirts or my clean ones? He said you would be a fool to give him your clean shirts. Dr. Hill said "you are right and you would be a fool to think that everyone that goes to church is clean. He said I would curse you out and I am not talking about before salvation or when I started preaching, I am talking about now. But I have not cursed anyone out this year I am getting better.

This whole story was to get him to see what Jesus was doing in this passage, to get us away from looking at others and to looking at the man in the mirror. So many people go to church and receive the word with joy but the moment they meet an offense they give up. The reason they were trapped is not due to the offender or their words but the condition of their heart. The focus is not to be but on others but that the light can shine on the condition of our hearts so not to be trapped by the enemy.

You can be wounded in humility but only offended with pride

Isaiah 55: ⁶*" Seek ye the* LORD *while he may be found, call ye upon him while he is near:* ⁷ *Let the wicked forsake his way, and the unrighteous man his thoughts: and let him return unto the* LORD*, and* *he will have mercy upon him; and to our God, for he will abundantly pardon. ⁸ For my thoughts are not your thoughts, neither are your ways my ways, saith the LORD."*

Pride always puts the spotlight on you and if it is on you it is off others and even God. While I was in Bible College there was a young woman that was in some of my classes at Fort Wayne Bible College now Taylor University. Whenever we had a class together, she would tell me how great of a dresser I was. To which I would always tell her thanks. God kept telling me to tell a girl that I was married. I could not see the purpose in doing something like that when I was not doing anything wrong. In addition, I liked the praise it might have stopped if I told her something stupid like that. Pride! This went on most of the semester and I liked it very much. One day we came into the class I sat in one of the many desks and said to my friend that this desk is getting smaller. She overheard the whole thing. My friend replied by saying the desk are not smaller you are getting fat. This girl did everything but hit my friend and had she not been restrained she might have done that as well.

Can you see where I am going with this? Because of my pride all this took place. Humility will recognize God's authority over your thinking. Pride ruled another time when God instructed me about the purchase of a building and property. We needed more space there was twelve acres of land and a fifty thousand square foot building. God told me to take the man out for breakfast telling him our intentions and then ask for the keys to begin renovations. I thought that God needed my help I was to prideful to ask this man just like that. I decided to tell him we would pay his asking price and give him a tax write off. To which he posed this question to me. He asked "had I heard of Alfonso Capone?" I said Al Capone he said yes and I said yes. He said "Al was of Italian decent and so am I, and ever since he made his mistake, every Italian wants to pay his taxes." He reached into his pocket took the keys out and passed them across the table to me. I felt so little because God knew the end in the beginning.

Offended people operate on rumors and partial truths not Kings

Matthew 18: [14] *"Even so it is not the will of your Father which is in heaven, that one of these little ones should perish.* [15] *Moreover if thy brother shall trespass against thee, go and tell him his fault between thee and him lone: if he shall hear thee, thou hast gained thy brother.* [16] *But if he will not hear thee, then take with thee one or two more, that in the mouth of two or three witnesses every word may be established.* [17] *And if he shall neglect to hear them, tell it unto the church: but if he neglect to hear the church, let him be unto thee as an heathen man and a publican.* [18] *Verily I say unto you, Whatsoever ye shall bind on earth shall be bound in heaven: and whatsoever ye shall loose on earth shall be loosed in heaven."*

Many times, we operate as if we were present when the event happens when we are really operating on what someone else said. One of my former Bishops shared with us one of his early mistakes he made in his ministry. He had poor judgment and had an affair. He was so broken by what he had done he considered suicide. He went into the woods to end it all and there God spoke to him and shared his love and forgiveness. He also promised him a very successful ministry if he would repent and not self-destruct. He did and God did. I am so glad that he did not stop because it was through his ministry I found the Lord. You must always remember that you are not an island to yourself, but many other people's lives intertwined into yours. God can forgive you, your life goes on but people and the rumor mill will continue. I want to say that I am sorry for his fall but grateful for his testimony. When I am confronted by the rumors, I was now fit to handle them. There are people who now know the story and they are putting their spin on it. He now is running around trying to correct the stories. This showed me how much God loves us in spite of us.

While he was in his church alone, an old woman came in and handed him a note and he bowed his head to read the note. When he looked up the woman was gone and he never saw her again. The note was in a language he would understand because of his love for the outdoors and hunting. It said quit chasing the devils rabbits. If you ever hunted rabbits, you know they are quick and move in all different directions. If you have a chance at one rabbit and then try to get another you might end up missing both. The thing that hurts you most when you have been offended is the rumor mill.

When I left my first ministry as I shared before in Fort Wayne Indiana, I was deeply hurt by people, my wife and I had served with our very lives. Nevertheless, remember some of these people were offended at our leaving. People can do you wrong but they do not want no one to leave them. Ever wonder why a man or woman who mistreats their mate but yet does not want to see them leave. That is just human nature and the deep selfish side of it. At the instruction of the Lord, we left and started in Tampa Florida. I was surprised at the rumors that spread. One was that I was dealing drugs and moved to Florida to get closer to my sources. Another one was, I went to court and was sentenced by the judge that either I would go to prison or should move to Florida, wow! With these rumors, spreading let us keep churning along. This woman said I was in a Texas prison. She was sharing the news with her coworker, but the coworker is my daughter and shares with her that she had spoken to me that morning and it was not from prison.

God gives us a solution to operating under these assumptions. He said if you were offended go to your brother. There is no one who understands what took place like the source. Kings do not operate on rumors. I can still remember a song I learned in kindergarten, it was" gossip, gossip evil thing much unhappiness it brings if you cannot say something nice don't talk at all is my advice". I thank my teacher Ms. Mitchell for teaching me that song it has been with me all these years. Offense will stop the work of the Kingdom and hinder what the plan of God is in your life. Go to your brother for the sole purpose of winning your brother not the argument. He said to tell him his fault and if he hears you, then you have won your brother, if he does not take two Elders and try to resolve the problem and if that does not work take him before the whole church.

Kingship Examination

Every level of growth produces new friends

1. True
2. False

Offense can cause you to be bitter and eventually defiled

1. True
2. False

Offense in the Greek means

1. Foolishness
2. Sin
3. Bait stick
4. None of the above

Offense in Latin means

1. Strong relationship
2. To strike out at something you believe in or trust
3. Get revenge
4. To hate the offender

Your tradition can cause you to be offended by the word of God

1. True
2. False

Your response to the offense is most important to God Matthew 13:20-21

1. True
2. False

You can be wounded in humility but only offended with pride

1. True
2. False

Pride takes the light off Christ and others

1. True
2. False

Offended people operate on rumors and partial truths, but not Kings

1. True
2. False

King to do list

- See have your friends grown with you
- Examine yourself for bitterness and ask why
- Are you trap by offense?
- What or who is causing you offense?
- How do you respond when offended?
- Do you have pride in your heart?
- What is more important to you how you feel or losing a friend?

Chapter Twelve

Reaching the Family

Kingdom life is much easier to live if the whole family is in it. So let's try to reach the family. For a background in this I want to use the fifth chapter of the Gospel of Mark. There are three people under the attack of the enemy in this chapter. First, there is a man in the tombs, there is a woman with the issue of blood, and there is a dead child. I do not believe it was an accident the way these stories were presented. I believe this is the strategy of the devil to destroy the work of the Kingdom in families. He first attacks the father who has great influence on the mother. Then because of the pressures of the parents, the children are dying.

The Husband is under attack

Mark 5: They went across the lake to the region of the Gerasenes.[a] ² When Jesus got out of the boat, a man with an impure spirit came from the tombs to meet him. ³ This man lived in the tombs, and no one could bind him anymore, not even with a chain. ⁴ For he had often been chained hand and foot, but he tore the chains apart and broke the irons on his feet. No one was strong enough to subdue him. ⁵ Night and day among the tombs and in the hills he would cry out and cut himself with stones. ⁶ When he saw Jesus from a distance, he ran and fell on his knees in front of him. ⁷ He shouted at the top of his voice, "What do you want with me, Jesus, Son of the Most High God? In God's name do not torture me!" ⁸ For Jesus had said to him, "Come out of this man, you impure spirit!" ⁹ Then Jesus asked him, "What is your name?" "My name is Legion," he replied, "for we are many." ¹⁰ And he begged Jesus repeatedly not to send them out of the area. ¹¹ A large herd of pigs was feeding on the nearby hillside. ¹² The demons begged Jesus, "Send us among the pigs; allow us to go into them." ¹³ He gave them permission, and the impure spirits came out and went into the pigs. The herd, about two thousand in number, rushed down the steep bank into the lake and were drowned. ¹⁴ Those tending the pigs ran off and reported this in the town and countryside, and the people went out to see what had happened. ¹⁵ When they came to Jesus, they saw the man who had been possessed by the legion of demons, sitting there, dressed and in his right mind; and they were afraid. ¹⁶ Those who had seen it told the people what had happened to the demon possessed man—and told about the pigs as well. ¹⁷ Then the people began to plead with Jesus to leave their region".

First line of attack: God's set authority

1 Corinthians 11: *³ But I want you to realize that the head of every man is Christ, and the head of the woman is man,[a] and the head of Christ is God".*

Whenever, you desire to destroy a thing start with the head. Satan saw this from the very beginning in the Garden of Eden. He started by getting man to disobey God. The other ploy you need to destroy a thing is to help it lose its purpose. Both of these things were accomplished in the garden. He started his attack at the head. I hear some say but he started with the woman and you are corrected. But woman is a part of the head. He made man male and female. A woman is a man with a womb she is a womb man. We talk to this later but whatever is given to a woman multiplies.

The second thing Satan did was to blind these two to their purpose a described in Genesis 1: *²⁶ Then God said, "Let us make mankind in our image, in our likeness, so that they may rule over the fish in the sea and the birds in the sky, over the livestock and all the wild animals,[a] and over all the creatures that move along the ground. "²⁷ So God created mankind in his own image, in the image of God he created them; male and female he created them. ²⁸ God blessed them and said to them, "Be fruitful and increase in number; fill the earth and subdue it. Rule over the fish in the sea and the birds in the sky and over every living creature that moves on the ground. "²⁹ Then God said, "I give you every seed-bearing plant on the face of the whole earth and every tree that has fruit with seed in it. They will be yours for food. ³⁰ And to all the beasts of the earth and all the birds in the sky and all the creatures that move along the ground—everything that has the breath of life in it—I give every green plant for food." And it was so. ³¹ God saw all that he had made, and it was very good. And there was evening, and there was morning—the sixth day.*

God create man to be ruler on the earth as he rules over them from the heavens. Satan understood the nature of the beast that we have a selfish self concern side. He was able to get man to think and to operate separate from God. Dr. Monroe put it so eloquent when he said that "everything that God made must stay connected to the place God created it to survive. Fish must remain in water plants and trees to the earth or they will die. God made man the only thing attached to him and he must remain there to live."

Man chose then and is still choosing to live without God. We have expelled him from our schools, and rule him unfit to serve in our government. We have replaced him with Psychology in our homes. We have deemed God unnecessary even in our churches. I heard this story of a preacher who came to town and wanted to preach at this church that had a conceded pastor. He promised the pastor that if he would allow him to preach that he would not mention God, Jesus or the Angels. But there are places like that now. God had given man directions to live this Kingdom life and that is simply put the word of the King or owner.

God has given man a Kingdom to rule over but like Satan and his Angels we want more than God has offered. We want to live independent of God. To shake off what thought was God's shackles we united against God and build a tower to escape in of his future judgment, and we all know what God did. God and man relationship got so bad that he said he was sorry he made man. What must he think today?

Look at what God had in mind and what we are today.

Psalms 8:1 Lord, *our Lord, how majestic is your*

name in all the earth! You have set your glory in the heavens. ²Through the praise of children and infants you have established a stronghold against your enemies, to silence the foe and the avenger. ³When I consider your heavens, the work of your fingers, the moon and the stars, which you have set in place, ⁴what is mankind that you are mindful of them, human beings that you care for them? [c] ⁵You have made them [d] a little lower than the angels [e] and crowned them [f] with glory and honor. ⁶You made them rulers over the works of your hands; ⁷all flocks and herds, and the animals of the wild, ⁸the birds in the sky, and the fish in the sea, all that swim the paths of the seas. ⁹LORD, our Lord, how majestic is your name in all the earth!

When we read this passage most of us who know what it mean usually jump to part where God describes us and fail to deal with our part. We are through our praises bring God to a stately acceptance upon the earth. God has according to this passage has given us a crown representing a Kingdom. He has made us in his image a little lower than the Angels Scholars say this is the word Elohim, not the regular word use to describe regular Angels, So God has design us to be gods on the earth notice but are to be submitted to the giver. I want to restate something here the only thing that God did not give man authority over is another man. So man has to submit himself to another man. Wives submit to your husband, this must be stated because she too is a ruler. For God's will to be carried out on earth some will have to submit to others under God. It is not a sign of weakness but strength through obedience. He said do everything as unto the Lord.

This being God's intention for man, let's look how far we have fallen. We have no intentions of bring God praise upon the earth we are too busy bring praise to ourselves. We like Lucifer have decided to do our own thing. Look at our demeanor on the earth and that of Lucifer in Isaiah 14: ¹²How you have fallen from heaven, *morning star, son of the dawn! You have been cast down to the earth, you who once laid low the nations!* ¹³ *You said in your heart, "I will ascend to the heavens; I will raise my throne above the stars of God; I will sit enthroned on the mount of assembly, on the utmost heights of Mount Zaphon.*[b]¹⁴ *I will ascend above the tops of the clouds; I will make myself like the Most High."* ¹⁵ *But you are brought down to the realm of the dead, to the depths of the pit.*

God like he did for man gave Lucifer a lofty position in his Kingdom. But it was not enough for him he wanted to have what was reserved for the creator. Most of us would deny that this too is what we want but our actions give us away. What were the things that Lucifer Wanted? All of his desires were to replace God, the same thing that we as men are doing today. We do not want God in our government are our schools and believe it or not even in our churches. A local church was having their business meeting when the pastor trying to bring order said brothers the Bible says when one of the deacons said do not come telling us about what that Bible says. We want God out when the plan was I will give you a place to rule in my Kingdom and you bring my praise to the earth. We want to rule yet without God. This man in our teaching is in the tombs demon possessed. Some men have discovered that we do not rule well by ourselves and have reached out for help still apart from God.

They have discovered that there is a spirit world and they have tapped into it for help. We know that there are spirits on this earth beside those of us that are in a body. Some of these spirits have been here for many years and have power beyond those of human strength. I was in to the martial arts and could do things with my body that was impossible in the natural but I was possessed by these spirits that gave me supernatural abilities.

There are people who have sold their souls to the devil in order to have these abilities. I was able to persuade people to do what I wanted with this power and that is what man wants more power less God. Somehow like me this man had opened himself up to the spirit world and is now controlled by it. I do not know what he did but I can give you some of the things that happen to me. I became fascinated with the spirit world as a young child. There was a cowboy show that the star would look for water with a wishbone stick. There were people who had séances and I remember me and my siblings trying to bring our grandfather back by trying what we had seen. Our father heard us came in and pretended to be him we came out from under that sheet scared to death. Then he told us never do that kind of thing again. Later in life I was attracted to drugs and pretty women both of which can be an avenue into the spirit world. The same Greek word for drugs is also the same for sorcery. In your Bible God would tell Israel to go in and destroy both men women and children? That use to sound so cruel to me until I realized he was trying to preserve the next generation form Idolatry pr demon worship. A complete turn from God is an inroad to becoming demon possess. If Satan is successful in his attack on the family structure starting with the man the child has no chance.

Let's look at some of the events around this man's life. Something developed in his pass to cause him to be here. Mark 8: *27 When Jesus stepped ashore, he was met by a demon possessed man from the town. For a long time this man had not worn clothes or lived in a house, but had lived in the tombs".*

Every one of us has had some pass events that must be dealt with are we too can be brought this low. I believe the actual event that open me up to the spirit world was the death of my father. My dad was a minister of the gospel. From the time of my birth all I knew was church as a child. It was as a child that I received the foundation to what I now do. My father grew up in a traditional church and I know that he and my mom loved God. I do believe that there were something's missing in our church like belief in God's supernatural ability to heal. My father died of cancer I was very hurt by this and blamed God. So many people who have been taught bad theology are bitter and now are wide open for the enemies attack. I do not know how many times I heard as a child that God was walking and looking for some flowers to put in his garden and chose someone's love one to place there.

When God tells us he came to bring life and that more abundantly. That Satan came to kill steal and destroy. We can open ourselves up to the devil by stargazing and astrology. So how exactly this man opens himself up we do not know. But we know that he did. Your past hurts must be dealt with and your past sins must be forgiven are you are a prime candidate for demon possession.

Secondly he lost his ability to deal with life death became an obsession.

Mark 5: ³ *This man lived in the tombs, and no one could bind him anymore, not even with a chain".*

Demons have no regard for human life. He leads the possess person to take on his personality. Have you notice the gangs of the inner cities use symbols to describe themselves that center around death. It is the same in the music industries they too focus on murder cop killings and other things that pertain to death. The most fascinating games our child likes to play are center around death. This man moved away from living things and was very content around death. The movie stars are in to conjuring up the dead. Our musicians utilize demon power to get and hold the record deals. These demons lead us away from that which produce and sustain life to things that don' produce or even destroy life. Look at God's warning to us concerning this time in 1 Timothy 4: *"The Spirit clearly says that in later times some will abandon the faith and follow deceiving spirits and things taught by demons. ² Such teachings come through hypocritical liars, whose consciences have been seared as with a hot iron. ³ They forbid people to marry and order them to abstain from certain foods, which God created to be received with thanksgiving by those who believe and who know the truth. ⁴ For everything God created is good, and nothing is to be rejected if it is received with thanksgiving, ⁵ because it is consecrated by the word of God and prayer".*

We are warned of what men would do in these last days. Notice the procession first they will leave the faith. The is a definite article designating one thing. There is only one name given under heaven that men might be saved and that is the name of Jesus. Man will be deceived. Deception can only come when one believe that what is told them is the truth. There was a game in street called three cards Monte and people believing they saw some would lose their money on that false belief. But in this case the stakes are higher and men will lose their souls. These spirits can do that which man cannot do and they will deceive men into believing that they are the truth. The deception will come through hypocrites. A hypocrite is one pretending to be what they are not. These demons will carry man to a place that he has no consciences. Marriage like it was at the time of Sodom and Gomorrah will become an issue. What is marriage who should or should not be married sound familiar. This is on our news every day as these demons rush to destroy what God has created and the man of this creation. The only way life can be produced is to follow God's pattern. Man wants to do his own thing and tell God to Butt out. So when man ventures out on his own trying to rule and reign without God this will always be the results.

Thirdly this man lost his original power and purpose

In Mark 5: *³ "This man lived in the tombs, and no one could bind him anymore, not even with a chain. ⁴ For he had often been chained hand and foot, but he tore the chains apart and broke the irons on his feet. No one was strong enough to subdue him. ⁵ Night and day among the tombs and in the hills he would cry out and cut himself with stones".*

This to me is one of the first prison cells. He with his entire God given gifts has to be separated from society to protect the life and possessions of others and sometime to protect him from himself. He was now no longer the King that God design but something that has been created by his owns selfishness and that of God's enemy Satan. Let's look at God's plan and that of the one he has embraced. In John 10: ¹⁰ "The thief comes only to steal and kill and destroy; I have come that they may have life, and have it to the full". His love for himself and his disregard for God's instruction has placed him in the hands of a hater. God desire for us is that we have life and that more abundantly. I research the word abundantly and the Greek word means in quantity and quality. Wow that is God's desire for his creature but we so many times choose that which makes us feel good or is more satisfying to our ego.

After making many foolish choices in his life let's look at the King David was mentoring King Solomon in Proverbs 14: *¹² There is a way that appears to be right, but in the end it leads to death". He give good advice also in proverbs 3: My son, do not forget my teaching, but keep my commands in your heart, ²for they will prolong your life many years and bring you peace and prosperity. ³ Let love and faithfulness never leave you; bind them around your neck, write them on the tablet of your heart. ⁴ Then you will win favor and a good name in the sight of God and man. ⁵ Trust in the LORD with all your heart and lean not on your own understanding; ⁶ in all your ways submit to him, and he will make your paths straight.[a]⁷ Do not be wise in your own eyes; fear the LORD and shun evil. ⁸ This will bring health to your body and nourishment to your bones".*

There are things that seem to be right but when we go down that road without God we find ourselves loosing. I can remember thinking as soon as I leave my father's house I am done with church. I did make that decision and went through with it. It hurt my mother's heart the decision I had made. She prayed for me and even threatens to through me in a hole at my death as you would do and animal. She said I did not go to church and she was not going to pretend at my death that I did. She was going to take me straight from the mortuary to the cemetery. I had made my choice and even those scary words were not going to change me. But it led me to doing things I never thought I could do the way I treated women and my own body was so foreign early in my life. I was taught to respect women but once exposed to the way the world did things it change me from the loving heart I had as a child to someone I did not even know. I remembered doing things and hurting people and returning to my home and look myself in the mirror and ask myself who are you. My doing my own thing led me to a place where I did not know me. I remember going to the little town I grew up in.

I was born in Mobile Alabama and live in through the fourth grade in Prichard. When I enter the fifth grade my dad moved us to his home town Mount Vernon Alabama. I went to that little town for a visit when I was still in that life without God. I remember one of my cousin who I loved very much, looking at me and asking me who was I. I was so hurt inside because we grew up together study together and I loved Mae Eva like she was my sister and to see her not being proud of me hurt. I shook it off and went on thinking she is just a square and I do not know what is happening. I moved from home at eighteen and up to live with a relative. I stayed with them for just over a month. I arrived in Fort Wayne, Indiana on July 4. Thank God now on August 17, I got my first real job and share a place with a friend for about a month and then got my own place. I was so use to being around family I end up marrying a beautiful girl both in and out. I met her through her sister who worked with me. I was eighteen years old and did not know anything about marriage. We were not taught things like that in our church. I remember doing a series on marriage in my church many years later and my mother was there. She was looking at me so attentively I was talking about sex in marriage and was a little embarrassed because of her presence.

Afterward I ask for questions or remarks her hand went up first I said o no. But what she said help to reiterate what I was telling you about me. This is what she said; I wished someone would have been taught these principles before we got married. Remember I had chosen to leave God out of my life it was one party after another. Believe it or not in my own selfish way I loved this girl but without God's help it was impossible to treat as such. So she finally had enough and divorced me I was devastated I did not believe in divorce and had lost my family. I since many times apologize to her for messing that part of her life up. I then began to arm myself to never be hurt again by a female. So I only let women get so close. I was evil because I was controlled by evil.

Even after I was saved and God gave me another chance and I met my present wife a beautiful young lady that lived down the street from me. I still after all these years sing a song to her that I sang back then. The song by the Temptations one of my favorite groups, went "each day through my window I watch her as she passes by and I say to myself you are such a lucky guy to have a girl like her is truly a dream come true out of all the fellows in the world she belong to you, but it was just my imagination running away with me". I use to watch her like that without saying anything. I want you to see the difference when you do it God's way.

After I was saved I had been in college two years without dating. I told God I wanted a wife not a girl friend and I believe you can show her to me tonight, it was 11:30 pm that night. The girl was not even saved and very worldly that is why I never approached her. But when I finished my prayer she knocked on my door. I can still remember opening the door and laughing out loud and saying the devil has messed with my prayers. She did get saved and filled with God's Spirit. We started to date and I had to beg God to teach me to love her because I did not know how. I did not know how important that prayer was because there have been situation in our lives that could have cause me to leave her but God's grave has been there. Her father given me advice on the day of our wedding said these words to me. There will be days you wished you had never seen this girl but do not bring her back here. It has been thirty-nine years by the help of the Lord and I never sent her back. I love her even more today than I did back then. See how far your life can get off track when you abundant God. This man lost his family and friends when these demons took over his life. Some of the smartest and most talented people I have ever met were behind bars or prison walls. God tells us that he set before us life and death and then said choose life.

Here is a list of things that a man needs to recover if he is to mentor or have and effect on the next generation.

1. Spiritual and human instinct - Lost while living among the dead

2. Supernatural strength from the right source - God instead of demons

3. The mind of Christ - Instead of demons that torment and cause self destruction

4. Help from the Holy Spirit - When before no one could control him

5. Follow the word of God and not superstition - When Jesus came to cast the demons out he called Jesus by his full name, the superstition of the that day said if you called a person by his full name you gain power over them

Fourth you must have a clean spirit to reach the next generation

> Mark 5: *⁶ When he saw Jesus from a distance, he ran and fell on his knees in front of him. ⁷ He shouted at the top of his voice, "What do you want with me, Jesus, Son of the Most High God? In God's name do not torture me!" ⁸ For Jesus had said to him, "Come out of this man, you impure spirit!" ⁹ Then Jesus asked him, "What is your name?" "My name is Legion," he replied, "for we are*

many." ¹⁰ *And he begged Jesus again and again not to send them out of the area.* ¹¹ *A large herd of pigs was feeding on the nearby hillside.*

Contrary to popular thought, demons do exist and they do possess people. I have already shared with you that the author at one time was demon possess. When Jesus met this man he was possessed by demon spirits. To say they do not exist is to call Jesus a liar. Demons again are spirits without a body always searching for a body to possess. When they find a willing agent they take over not only their body but their personality. This man had open himself up for take over and take over they did. The man saw Jesus as a way out and we must as well.

The process of a clean spirit

1. Submit to a stronger force: Mark 5: ⁶ When he saw Jesus from a distance, he ran and fell on his knees in front of him.

2. Worshipful atmosphere will expose demons: Mark 5: ⁷ He shouted at the top of his voice, "What do you want with me, Jesus, Son of the Most High God? In God's name do not torture me!"

3. Your condition properly diagnosed: Mark 5: ⁸ For Jesus had said to him, "Come out of this man, you impure spirit!"

4. Someone who operates in the authority of God: Mark 5: ⁹ Then Jesus asked him, "What is your name?"

"My name is Legion," he replied, "for we are any."

¹⁰ And he begged Jesus again and again not to send them out of the area. ¹¹ A large herd of pigs was feeding on the nearby hillside. ¹² The demons begged Jesus, "Send us among the pigs; allow us to go into them." ¹³ He gave them

permission, and the impure spirits came out and went into the pigs. The herd, about two thousand in number, rushed down the steep bank into the lake and were drowned.

5. Changes both spirit and soul: Mark 5: [14] Those tending the pigs ran off and reported this in the town and countryside, and the people went out to see what had happened. [15] When they came to Jesus, they saw the man who had been possessed by the legion of demons, sitting there, dressed and in his right mind; and they were afraid.

6. Your change affects others: Mark 5: [16] Those who had seen it told the people what had happened to the demon possessed man—and told about the pigs as well. [17] Then the people began to plead with Jesus to leave their region.

[18] As Jesus was getting into the boat, the man who had been demon possessed begged to go with him. [19] Jesus did not let him, but said, "Go home to your own people and tell them how much the Lord has done for you, and how he has had mercy on you." [20] So the man went away and began to tell in the Decapolis[b] how much Jesus had done for him. And all the people were amazed.

Listen to David after he had allowed the devil to entice him to have sex with another man's wife and then have the man killed. When the prophet confronted him he did not become defensive but acknowledged his wrong and pleaded to God for help. What did he want from God? He wanted to be clean again so he could live the right way.

Psalms 51: [1] Have mercy on me, O God, according to your unfailing love; according to your great compassion blot out my transgressions. [2] Wash away all my iniquity and cleanse me from my sin. [3] For I know my transgressions, and my sin is always before me. [4] Against you, you only, have I sinned and done what is evil in your sight; so you are right in your verdict and justified when you judge. ⁵ Surely I was sinful at birth, sinful from the time my mother conceived me. ⁶ Yet you desired faithfulness even in the womb; you taught me wisdom in that secret place. ⁷ Cleanse me with hyssop, and I will be clean; wash me, and I will be whiter than snow. ⁸ Let me hear joy and gladness; let the bones you have crushed rejoice. ⁹ Hide your face from my sins and blot out all my iniquity. ¹⁰ Create in me a pure heart, O God, and renew a steadfast spirit within me. ¹¹ Do not cast me from your presence or take your Holy Spirit from me. ¹² Restore to me the joy of your salvation and grant me a willing spirit, to sustain me. ¹³ Then I will teach transgressors your ways, so that sinners will turn back to you.

David knew that because of his spirit that something had happen to him. Let's look at what he desired from God.

- He desired God's mercy
- With love blot out my sins
- He wanted God's judgment because it was God's law he broke
- He wanted to be clean again
- He wanted to be pure in heart and to be faithful again
- He wanted God's presence
- He wanted joy so he could share with others

Kingship Examination

It is important to reach your family

    1. True

    2. False

According to 1 Corinthians 11:3 who is the head of the house

    1. The woman

    2. The man

    3. The child

    4. The boss

In Genesis 1:26 God authority to man

    1. True

    2. False

Through Praise we can bring stately acceptance of God to the earth

    1. True

    2. False

According to Psalms 8:5 we were made a little lower than God

    1. True

    2. False

Mar 8 warns us that demons can possess a man

1. True
2. False

A possessed person will have an affinity to death

1. True
2. False

Rebellion against God and his leadership can cause us to lose the power and authority he gave us

1. True
2. False

King to do list

- Make certain your actions line up with the word of God
- Make certain you are being led by the Spirit and not driven by demons
- Life is more important to you than death
- Stay in a right relation with God
- Make reaching your family a priority
- Become a praise
- To mentor

1. You must have spiritual and human instinct
2. God's power
3. The mind of Christ
4. The Holy Spirit's Guidance
5. Know the word of God 6.

Chapter Thirteen

The Woman Under Attack

The wo-man the man with a womb' Dr. Myles Monroe in one of his teachings talked about anything you give a woman multiplies. This is the reason she is a man with a womb. The devil is a shrewd being. He attacks the man because of God placing him as head of the family. In the same way, he attacks the woman because there would be no life without her womb.

Let us look at his attack against this woman in the gospel of Mark. Mark 5: *[25] "And a woman was there who had been subject to bleeding for twelve years. [26] She had suffered a great deal under the care of many doctors and had spent all she had, yet instead of getting better she grew worse. [27] When she heard about Jesus, she came up behind him in the crowd and touched his cloak, [28] because she thought, "If I just touch his clothes, I will be healed." [29] Immediately her bleeding stopped and she felt in her body that she was freed from her suffering. [30] At once Jesus realized that power had gone out from him. He turned around in the crowd and asked, "Who touched my clothes?" [31] "You see the people crowding against you," his disciples answered, "and yet you can ask, 'Who touched me?' "*

[32] But Jesus kept looking around to see who had done it. [33] Then the woman, knowing what had happened to her, came and fell at his feet and, trembling with fear, told him the whole truth. [34] He said to her, "Daughter, your faith has healed you. Go in peace and be freed from your suffering."

- The woman bled for twelve years: According to Wikipedia, "menstrual cycle is the cycle of changes that occurs in the uterus (womb) and ovary (egg) for the purpose of sexual reproduction. It is essential for the production of eggs and for the preparation of the uterus (womb) for pregnancy." So bleeding in a woman is important to bring and carry the next generation. So in order to stop the progress it would be important to an enemy either to stop the flow or to increase the flow. In this woman's case, the devil increased her flow for twelve years.

Results of her bleeding

1. Preparation but no conception or delivery. The devil has a lot of us in this place. We are constantly preparing to do something but never able to deliver. How many times have you told yourself you were going to get back in church and work for the Kingdom or that you were going back to school and finish your education. Others plan to start a business or write a book or start some other career. However, many of us find ourselves like this woman bleeding always preparing to do something but never getting around to doing it.

   I want to encourage you to stop bleeding and finish what you started. This poor woman for twelve years was preparing her body to conceive and to bring forth a child but never able to carry it out. This is a work of the devil to keep us busy preparing until time runs out and we are unable to do so. We all know that without God intervening there is a limited amount of time for a woman to become pregnant and bring forth a child. There is also an expiration date on your dreams and vision. You need to do what this woman did and get the help of the Lord to do what you in your natural state cannot do.

2. The number twelve: She was sick for twelve years. Twelve is the number of a perfect government for example there were twelve disciples, there were twelve tribes of Israel. We put twelve on the Jury. This was a mockery of her potential as a ruler upon the earth

and a producer of rulers. God in Genesis 1 gave man authority upon the earth. The devil tricked man out of his rightful place by convincing man that he could do this without God. Only when we as this woman did return to God will we be put back in our rightful place. God placed you on this earth and has given you the authority. We have allowed our circumstance to keep us back. God said of his Kingdom that the government would be on his shoulders this is a part of the body not the head. You are seated together with Christ. Christ sits on a throne, a place of authority and that means you are seated on a throne. Like this woman, we are not reaching our God given potential because of preparation without the ability to reach success.

The problem is that we are trying to reach this without God. God said that if my people who are called by name would humble themselves and pray that he would hear and heal our land. The problem in our cities is an absence of the man; he is consumed with death so he cannot deal with the problems of life. The woman because of the absence of the man is bleeding, she is full of potential but she cannot conceive. What is your excuse that you are not standing in your rightful place in God? Most of us are in the church but not in Christ. We are like the religious people of old. Jesus went to his own hometown and could not do many miracles because of their unbelief. To quote a great man of God of this time Dr. T.L. Osborne "sin consciousness destroys faith in God, in the Bible in others and most of all in one's self. This sense of inadequacy discourages initiative. It engenders an inferiority complex. One becomes snared by negativism and lives with a sense of condemnation, in fear of God, searching for someone else to pray for them, because of their own sense of indignity and ignominy before God." When you have not understood your place in God the devil keeps you looking at what you do not have. Just as Dr. Osborne says, it destroys your initiative. There is no drive because you have not focused on the right thing.

3. She is Divorced: Under Hebrew law she is divorced, not because of her own choosing but because of her condition. In her case, she cannot be near a man because she would contaminate him and he would be considered unclean. There are many women in this condition today, divorced by no choice of their own but because of circumstance. Some are divorced because of the condition of the man he is in the graveyard embracing death. Death can come in many ways. Remember the scripture that said there is a way that seems right unto man but the end is destruction. Death can be in the form of religion and not a living relationship. When there is ignorance of the word of God, man replaces what they do not know with do's and don'ts. My main reason for not wanting to go to church was not that I did not want a relationship with God. We were raised to think God did not want you to enjoy life; we could not play ball on Sunday or any games with a dice.

Religion kills and destroys the morale of people who desire God. A funny story to show what I mean. When we were very young, my brother and I were in church. Our Pastor had finished his message and was having people to come join the church. That was the way it was done in our church, we were not invited to receive Christ but to join the church. God was tugging at my heart and if joining the church would get me right with him, I wanted it. I was afraid to go up front by myself so I lied to my brother and told him momma said she was going to whip us if we did not join the church, when we were eating he was trying to ask momma did she say that. He had a stammering tongue at that time so I cut him off before he could finish and got him out to play. This kind of death led me to another I was going to live without God. I turned to as much sex as possible drugs, alcohol, even sports and many other vices, but death is death. Some of our men have turned to crime and have landed in prison; others have turned to other men. So bleeding women have few choices when it comes to men. It is not all the man's fault it is sometimes the bleeding woman. Some women have been alone for a while and cannot give up their freedom even when married. Others are completely ignorant of the will of God in marriage.

4. No fellowship: She is not only separated from her husband, but from other women in the synagogue. The Bible teaches that iron sharpens iron. It is through others that we learn. One writer told us that no man is an island to himself. I have watched people over the years destroy relationships not knowing they may need that same person later. I can remember being mistreated by a family member who had to live with me later in life twice. I discovered that the greatest thing in the Kingdom is relationship.

The Kingdom is built on it. God said to love God and love man, this is the Kingdom. The disciples were excited that demons were subject to them. Jesus told them to be more excited that their names were written in the book of life. When you do not understand relationship, you do not understand God. He said how could you love me, in whom you have not seen, and hate your brother. One of the greatest punishments hell will bring is to be alone. When a prisoner is given the ultimate punishment, he is placed in solitary confinement. This woman for twelve years was in solitary confinement. Some of you that are reading this book are now in solitary confinement. Some of you, in order to please a man have separated yourself from your family friends and even God. However, while you are there your bleeding continues and there is no one to touch to bring you out. It is time for you to join the Kingdom again, do not delay do it today.

5. Undue suffering with financial disaster: this woman had did all she knew to do to get well. She had gone to doctors and was only taken advantage of. I am reminded of my first year in college; there was a pancake restaurant across the street from my school. I went there to study and to eat. This particular day I was studying the book of Revelation and was approached by the waitress and asked what was I reading. When I told her, she said no one could understand that, to which I replied yes you can. When she left to place, my order God told me to witness to her and tell her about him. I was not to stop her work but write her a letter and give it to her and I did. She went in the back read my letter returned with a question. She asked could I come and talk to her after she was off from work. I said I would and did.

Remember the life I came out of I am newly saved and she was strikingly beautiful. When we sat to talk she opened up by saying I am a nymph. This was March she said I have had more than forty men from the beginning of the year, and I do not know most of their names. On top of this, she was married. She told me I will make advances at you I cannot help it. When you look at this girl, you would be afraid to talk to her because of her beauty. She was blond with blue eyes and had a very fit body. She went further to say that she had searched out help from counselors and pastors and that they all slept with her. I was smart enough to know that I was unable to do this alone. I asked her to give me a chance to run across the street. I went and got one of my professors to come and witness with me. We led her to the Lord and years later, she sent a message to me that she was still walking with the Lord. She like this woman was searching for help and went through undue suffering trying to find her way out. There are some of you right now looking to get out and going farther in. One of the things I did in the ministry in Fort Wayne was to buy a house to use to help women who really wanted out and had a place to stay. I told you I lived the life of a pimp and knew that some of these girls were trapped trying to leave an abusive father only to get an abusive pimp. In your tutoring try to identify with the person and understand their background, if not you can become a part of the problem.

Change cause for desperate measures: *Mark 5:* [27] *"When she heard about Jesus, she came up behind him in the crowd and touched his cloak,* [28] *because she thought, "If I just touch his clothes, I will be healed."*

Salvation or deliverance begins with a word. This woman heard about Jesus. Paul in his letter to the Romans wrote that faith comes by hearing and hearing by the word of God. I want to say this again because of its importance's, faith comes by hearing. The reason our children are so involved in sex or crimes is that their music is filled with it. Girls are told to back that thang up, after a while you will do it. Drop it like it's hot after a while it's hot and dropping. Faith comes by what you keep hearing; true faith comes by hearing the word of God. This is why the great commission is so important; people need to hear that Jesus can help them.

Every action you do starts with a word either one someone says or one that originates in you but it started with a word. This woman heard a word about the healing ministry of Jesus and took desperate measures to obtain it. Remember she is unclean, is not to appear in public, and definitely is not to touch anyone especially a Rabbi. Nevertheless, her condition calls for these kind of measures. I heard for years that when you get sick and tired of being sick and tired you would do whatever it takes to get free. I was told this story of an African Sage that was approached by a young man to discover the secret of being successful. He asked old man his question about life, to which came no reply. He ask again in disgust and the old man got up took him by the hand led him to a body of water and walked in. He walked out until the water was over his head stood a while and then walked out went back to his chair and sat down. The boy still did not understand and ask him again. The old man ask the young man when we were under the water what did you want the most he said to breath. The old man told him when you desire success like that you will get it. He was saying you need to be desperate. The wonderful story of Queen Esther in the Bible teaches this principle. She had to go before the King without an invitation for the salvation of her people. She understood if he did not extend his staff to her, she was dead. She saw the problem bigger than her life and said if I perish, I perish. The lepers outside the walls were face with a desperate situation no food and death a certainty they decided to put their life on the line and go to the enemy's camp. Through their desperation, they were saved and so was the city. This woman knew what her end could be if she had misjudged Jesus and he was like one of the Pharisees. Thank God, he was not and she got her miracle I do not care what your condition is you can approach Jesus and get your miracle.

- See your change: *Mark 5:* [28]*" because she thought, "If I just touch his clothes, I will be healed."* [29] *Immediately her bleeding stopped and she felt in her body that she was freed from her suffering."*

Jesus said when you pray believe that you receive and you will have it. He told us to ask for what we desire. Yet many of us pray our problems not what we desire. Pray your desire not your problem. Mark said her thoughts motivated her not her condition. She thought if I could just touch, I would be healed. The miracle came because she made her mind speak what was in her heart and her miracle came. We are taught that as a man thinks so is he. So to reach our goals we need to first see ourselves free and then speak what we see. We need to get the bleeding woman back in life and developing life in others.

Kingship Examination

Bleeding was ever being prepared without success.

　1. True

　2. False

Twelve is the number of perfect government.

　1. True

　2. False

Her separation was to protect others from defilement.

　1. True

　2. False

She can go to the Temple.

　1. True

　2. False

Her decision to touch Jesus placed her life in danger.

　1. True

　2. False

Change calls for life altering decision.

　1. True

　2. False

King to do list

- Prepare, Expect, perform to get results
- Stand in Kingdom authority for victory
- Separation from other may be a priority
- Put your life behind your faith
- Embrace change

Chapter Fourteen
The Child

The child: Mark 5: [19] *Jesus did not let him, but said, "Go home to your own people and tell them how much the Lord has done for you, and how he has had mercy on you." And all the people were amazed.*

Jesus Raises a Dead Girl and Heals a Sick Woman

Mark 5:21 "When Jesus had again crossed over by boat to the other side of the lake, a large crowd gathered around him while he was by the lake. [22] *Then one of the synagogue leaders, named Jairus, came, and when he saw Jesus, he fell at his feet.* [23] *He pleaded earnestly with him, "My little daughter is dying. Please come and put your hands on her so that she will be healed and live."* [24] *So Jesus went with him. A large crowd followed and pressed around him.* [25] *And a woman was there who had been subject to bleeding for twelve years."*

We have seen the man in the tombs and the woman sick in the streets. After the healing of the man, Jesus is approached by a concerned father. His child is at home sick unto death. I like what the great Baptist preacher Dr. C.A.W. Clark said concerning Jairus request for Jesus. "He said when Jairus requested that Jesus respond, he did not always do that sometimes he puts you on hold yea". On the way to the ruler's house Jesus was faced with another problem the woman in the street. I want us to look at the progression of this story and I do not believe that the Holy Spirit made a mistake in the order of these stories. If you have a man out of place and a woman consumed with sickness, there is nothing left to happen but the death of the child. The whole family is under attack and all need a touch from the Lord.

Jesus was delayed: Mark 5:[23] *"He pleaded earnestly with him, "My little daughter is dying. Please come and put your hands on her so that she will be healed and live."* [24] *So Jesus went with him."* A large crowd followed and pressed around him. [25] And a woman was there who had been subject to bleeding for twelve years.

Jairus had gotten and audience with Jesus and his consent to come and heal the child but now he is interrupted by a sick woman in the street. Dr. Clark would say, "That need for the woman was greater because she was sick in the street and that the little girl was sick at home with her mother watching at her bedside and if your imagination is working you see her there". Nevertheless, for whatever the reason he is delayed to minister to the woman in the street. There was a song that was sung in the church I grew up in it went something like this "Job was sick so long until the flesh fell from his bones, his wife, cattle and children everything that he had was gone but Job he did not fret he said God has never fail me yet, he may not come when you want him but he is right on time." I do believe that God is always on time. I had a young woman in my church in Fort Wayne that was gifted in singing. We were praying for God to use her greatly.

I had some very important people in the industry come and sing at our church. I remember one in particular he was a great friend and Godfather to my son Jonathan. His name was Jessy Dixon a powerful worshiper for God. I remember asking him about taking her with him and this is what he said to me. (This girl is gifted and is not a backup singer and I am not about to let her sing before me.) I would tell her not now, it does not mean never. I remember preaching in Nigeria, and the driver put a CD in and I told him to turn the music up, it was my girl, she was now being played around the world. Delay sometimes means God is adding to your destiny. Look how long Joseph, Moses, Joshua and David had to wait before they walked into their destiny.

Just because you had plans for yesterday maybe tomorrow will be better. There is something else about the story I believe we can learn. Remember Jesus had just return from healing the man in the tombs. I believe that people were the same then as they are today so surely this man heard of the miracle in the tombs. Then now he is there to witness what happens to the woman in the street. Both of these things will give his faith to believe that Jesus is now able to perform the miracle he needs. I was preaching in London, there were other speakers, and as they spoke, I must confess that I heard very little. My mind was back in the states focusing on a need of twenty thousand dollars I needed. Then a young Nigerian singer sadly I do not remember her name but I will never forget what she sang. The song was if he did it before he will do it again. I started remembering all the miracles God had performed for me, one I was building a new church in Fort Wayne Indiana. There was a great man in my church that I had great respect for. He asked me to give his son an opportunity to be the builder of the church. I was not afraid of his ability to build because he had learned that from his father. I was afraid because he did not have his father's integrity. Reluctantly I consented to his building of the church; his bid came in lower than all the others did. We tried to cover our tracts and we had a no lien contract.

I had a faithful young woman working for me in my office but because of my schedule, I allowed her to fill out the paper work. Her not being aware of legal matters did not put our full name on the contract. Just as I thought this young man had under bided to get the job.

Therefore, when he was given the check he was not paying his sub-contractors. There was no way I could use the money because the check was written to him. He in his own defense told the contractors that I was not paying him and he was even able to produce tears for one who told me he hated me for my action. The banks who handled all of the checks knew what had happen and called a meeting with the contractors. He told them that there was no way I could use the money and that he knew that the general contractor had lied. He told them because of the integrity of the pastor he was willing, being the chief lien holder to offer them twenty-nine cent on the dollar. They could take that or he would foreclose on me and sell the building back to me the next day.

God brought me out. So listening to this girl, I was convinced God would do it again. Not only did God do it but also he had someone that was on the trip with me to write out the whole check. Delay does not mean failure.

Victory comes when you focus only on what God is saying: *Mark 5:* [34] *He said to her, "Daughter, your faith has healed you. Go in peace and be freed from your suffering."* [35] *While Jesus was still speaking, some people came from the house of Jairus, the synagogue leader. "Your daughter is dead," they said. "Why bother the teacher anymore?"* [36] *Overhearing[c] what they said, Jesus told him, "Don't be afraid; just believe."*

To get a victory you must know the voice and the will of the master. Jesus said that his sheep hear his voice and another they will not follow. The church that I just shared with you was a miracle within itself. Where God showed me to build was right in the middle of the city. He had me to start buying a lot at a time. If that was all, it would not be that much but there were properties in the middle that were private homes and some owned by the county and both were saying that they had no intention of selling. I can still remember carrying a group from our church to march and pray around the property. Some actually laughed at me aloud and said, how can you build here when these people said no? My response was always that God said. It was also when Jimmy Carter was President and the interest rates on money were sky high. Nevertheless, little by little the land became available until we had it all, to God be the glory.

I believe I shared the story earlier I was on the way to prayer meeting in Los Angeles on a bicycle at 5 am, when God asked me about being his witness. He explained that I was always in court and that I was the one on the witness stand.

God the father sits as Judge, Jesus is my defense attorney and that Satan is the prosecutor. He said that everything I said on the stand would be cross-examined by the prosecutor. He reminded me that just before his death that Peter testified that he would be willing to die for him. How he was told that before morning you will be cross-examined for your testimony, and we all know what happened there. This man had a word from the Lord, a new word will not change the first word you have from him no matter how severe it sounds. Jesus told him not to fear only believe. I by the Holy Spirit am telling someone with some terrible news not to fear only believe.

Have someone around that you can trust with your life: *Mark 5:* [37] *"He did not let anyone follow him except Peter, James and John the brother of James."*

Jesus had twelve disciples but only three were present in severe instances. You must have some people around you that they themselves are close to God. I had just returned from Managua and Matagalpa Nicaragua, we were ministering to a group of pastors in preparation for an Evangelistic outreach plan by Pastor Nolan Edwards and Champion Church of Winter Haven Florida. On this trip was Pastor Nolan the leader, Pastor Paul Pickern, and myself. Pastor Nolan with the help of the Holy Spirit chose this group because we had minister in Kenya, East Africa together. We know each other's strengths and weakness but we also know our love for God and for each other. We flow together and minister well together. This does not mean there are no disagreements we had ours.

Yet we know that we can trust one another. The word remains the same but methods can differ. There was an occasion where under pressure one person blew up but the other two remained calm because we understood. The reason I shared this story is because sometimes we are looking for someone perfect to do ministry with and there is no such creature. Jesus did not take these three with him because of their perfection but because of their maturity and relationship. If you remember that, you are not perfect it will help you in developing the right people to be in your inner circle. Remember as you look at your inner circle you are looking at your tomorrow.

My mother would tell us that birds of a feather flock together. When I was young, I did not know what she was talking about. I have lived longer enough to understand she was telling me to choose my friends carefully because I will become if not already one of them. It is not enough that they are in the church but that Christ is in and working through them. There are minister that are associates but not close friends because of their life style. If you make a decision to go the way of the Lord, make certain that your friends are too. I remember a friend that he and I would leave the city drive out in the countryside smoke marijuana and solve all the world's problems. When we met, again, I had given my life to Christ and we could only greet one another and move on.

Here are some things I believe are very important in choosing friends. Number one, that they have a relationship with your father, both heavenly and earthly. Notice I said both fathers your God and the one who will help you stay close to him your pastor. When your friend talks negatively about either, it will affect you. I wrote a book on church spirits and one I discussed the spirit of defamation. This spirits goal is to shut the mouth of the one being defamed and to cause others not to listen. Paul said I am evil spoken of yet the word of God is not bound. Paul was aware of this spirit's purpose in his life and would not allow its success. Paul said in spite of what is being said about me I am still preaching.

The young people call them haters and that is exactly what they are. They hate the call of God on your life and the destiny God has laid out for you. Number two, you need to have the same goals. The Bible says how two can walk together except they agree. If your friend is not going the same way, they will not understand your destiny. Next, they should have the same passion in reaching your destiny. Even though Jesus chose these men, they did not always share his passion. He took them to pray with him doing the most decisive time in his ministry and he found them asleep.

'Yet they understood better than the rest and they were what I discovered in an acronym F.A.T., Faithful, Available and Teachable. If these attributes are not in your companions leave them behind. I had some associates that brag on the point that they were un-teachable, I had to move on. I believe this is why Jesus chose Peter, James and John; they were with him when things were desperate and when there was new revelation coming out. He took them with him to raise the young woman from the dead. I believe that they could grow to the next level of maturity. Remember later in the book of Acts they told a cripple man they had something, it was the name of Jesus. I believe their time with Jesus was the reason for their success.

Holiness before Miracles: *Mark 5:*³⁷ *"He did not let anyone follow him except Peter, James and John the brother of James.* ³⁸ *When they came to the home of the synagogue leader, Jesus saw a commotion, with people crying and wailing loudly.* ³⁹ *He went in and said to them, "Why all this commotion and wailing? The child is not dead but asleep."* ⁴⁰ *But they laughed at him. After he put them all out, he took the child's father, mother and the disciples who were with him, and went in where the child was."*

This would be foreign to most us living in the west but very common to those of Jesus' day. These people gathered here were not all family but were hired by the family to come and morn the deceased. The richer the family the more mourners you could hire. This was to show how much the deceased was loved and would be missed. Therefore, when Jesus arrived and spoke a word of faith that cannot be heard by unbelievers they stop mourning to ridicule his statement. Remember they were not true mourners but hired. Jesus had all of them removed before going forward with the miracle.

There are things in our lives that make fun of the word

of God that must be removed before your destiny can be fulfilled. It may be as we were previously teaching a friend. It could be a habit or some foreign god you have in your heart or house. Whatever the person or thing that keeps you from believing the word of the Lord, it must be removed. I had some amulets in my house also signs of the zodiac that had to be removed before I could walk in my destiny. Let the Holy Spirit examine your heart for what needs to be removed and then go in boldly for your miracle. When you do, those on the borderline of a miracle will go in with you. Jesus not only took the disciples but the girl's parents too. The book of Romans teaches that all creation is waiting on the manifestation of the sons of God. In other words, others can become believers by watching God work through you.

Lesson taught by Jesus: *Mark 5: [41] "He took her by the hand and said to her, "Talitha koum!" (which means "Little girl, I say to you, get up!"). [42] Immediately the girl stood up and began to walk around (she was twelve years old). At this, they were completely astonished."*

The victory comes from the heart through the mouth. Jesus also taught this to his disciples in Mark 11: [20] *In the morning, as they went along, they saw the fig tree withered from the roots.* [21] *Peter remembered and said to Jesus, "Rabbi, look! The fig tree you cursed has withered!"* [22] *"Have faith in God," Jesus answered.* [23] *"Truly[] I tell you, if anyone says to this mountain, 'Go, throw yourself into the sea,' and does not doubt in their heart but believes that what they say will happen, it will be done for them.* [24] *Therefore I tell you, whatever you ask for in prayer, believe that you have received it, and it will be yours.* [25] *And when you stand praying, if you hold anything against anyone, forgive them, so that your Father in heaven may forgive you your sins."*

When Jesus had approached this tree and there was no fruit, he cursed it. When the disciples saw it the next day they were astonished and told Jesus so. Jesus took that opportunity to teach the same lesson found in Mark 5, the power of the authoritative tongue. He taught that if you do not doubt you can have what you say. The most of us have learned to pray but few of us understand the power of the spoken word. I encourage you to speak to your problems, it can hear you. Jesus spoke to the wind and it obeyed him. He did not pray to it he spoke to it. Jesus spoke to the little girl and she got up. The Bible tells us that our authority is not limited to this earth but under and above it. When Jesus spoke to the little girl, the real person had left the body. Nevertheless, he knew it was not limited to the earth but to whatever place the little girl's spirit was and he had authority there as well and so do you. I encourage you to open up your mouth and speak.

Jesus final instruction to the parents: Mark 5:[43] *"He gave strict orders not to let anyone know about this, and told them to give her something to eat".*

Make no place for the devil; do not tell anyone and you need to feed the child. How many people have received the miracle of salvation but were exposed to quickly to the enemies trap and ended up back in the world. When I was saved many wanted me to share my testimony, I knew I was not ready so I kept quiet until I was strong enough. The second thing was to give her something to eat. We sometimes see many people saved but no one feeds them and they get weak and return to the world. Jesus said go into the entire world and preach the gospel teaching them to observe all I have commanded. Once you have been mentored, you are to mentor others. Do not leave a baby to nourish itself but take on the responsibility to feed them. Jesus told Peter to feed the sheep and the lambs. Lambs and sheep must be fed.

Kingship Examination

Victory comes from God's word.

1. True
2. False

You need victory partners.

1. True
2. False

Sanctification is a prerequisite of your miracles.

1. True
2. False

Your mouth exposes your heart.

1. True
2. False

Miracle recipients need protection and nourishment.

1. True
2. False

King to do list

- Confess God's word daily
- Develop victory partners
- Clean-up to go up

Be cautious about sharing your miracle

Chapter Fifteen
Time and Attitude

Attitude determines Altitude: Philippians 4: *"Therefore, my brothers and sisters, you whom I love and long for, my joy and crown, stand firm in the Lord in this way, dear friends!* [2] *I plead with Euodia and I plead with Syntyche to be of the same mind in the Lord.* [3] *Yes, and I ask you, my true companion, help these women since they have contended at my side in the cause of the gospel, along with Clement and the rest of my co-workers, whose names are in the book of life.* [4] *Rejoice in the Lord always. I will say it again: Rejoice!* [5] *Let your gentleness be evident to all. The Lord is near.* [6] *Do not be anxious about anything, but in every situation, by prayer and petition, with thanksgiving, present your requests to God.* [7] *And the peace of God, which transcends all understanding, will guard your hearts and your minds in Christ Jesus.* [8] *Finally, brothers and sisters, whatever is true, whatever is noble, whatever is right, whatever is pure, whatever is lovely, whatever is admirable—if anything is excellent or praiseworthy—think about such things.* [9] *Whatever you have learned or received or heard from me, or seen in me— put it into practice. And the God of peace will be with you."*

The Apostle Paul in his letter to the Philippians was very detail in his effort to aid these Christians in their walk with the Lord.

- **He dealt with their mindset**- Having the same mindset, as those you work with will deal a destructive blow to contention. Two women in the church were at odds with each other, Paul was instructing the leaders to bring them together. Wars began with each having an opinion and desire to have what the other has. When the attitude is that of serving the Kingdom it ends strife. He told them to rejoice in the Lord always. To re do anything is to do it again. Joy is not the result of something positive happening but being in a positive state that is in Christ. Happiness is the result of a happening but the Joy of the Lord is our strength.

- **Your mind cannot be filled with anxiousness and fear**; we have a place to carry our concern. Christ does not want you to carry your burdens but to cast them on him. So we are instructed to pray and to make our request known unto God. We have to learn contentment it is not automatic when you give your life to Christ. Paul said I have learned to be content in whatsoever state I am in. Therefore, we are to approach prayer with a grateful heart, thanking God for what he has already done. Something will take place in you that cannot be explain by natural means. We end up having peace and still yet have the same problems. The way you will know that God has your request is that you have a peace about it. When you are fretting about your problem, you still possess it. God's peace is the way you know that he is moving on your behalf.

- **Garbage in garbage out**: Philippians 4: ^{8}"Finally, brothers and sisters, whatever is true, whatever is noble, whatever is right, whatever is pure, whatever is lovely, whatever is admirable—if anything is excellent or praiseworthy—think about such things. ^{9}Whatever you have learned or received or heard from me, or seen in me—put it into practice. And the God of peace will be with you."

Paul teaches us something we learn from programming computers, what you put in you will get out.

He said these thoughts should fill your mind

    1. What is true - will expose false

2. What is noble/honest - will expose a lie

3. What is right- will expose wrong

4. Pure - expose the defile

5. Lovely - expose wrong motive

6. Good report or admirable - bad report

7. Things that are praise worthy - destroy false worship

Paul instructs us to only think on these things. Most mental illness is a result of bad thinking. Let us free our mind and think on these things.

In this final chapter, I want to talk directly to your heart as a leader. I shared with you earlier about Pastor Green a wonderful woman of God. She was the pastor of a little church around the corner from my large church. I do not know if she is still on earth or in the presence of God but she saved my life. I want to repay her and the Lord for sending her my way. I was young, energetic and foolish. I was so caught up in making things right for the years I wasted before Christ. I worked long taxing hours away from my home and family; sound familiar. I wanted to make a difference and did. However, the cost was over whelming. The words this little woman brought me transformed my life and ministry. She simply said, "God did not tell you to die for these people he did". I was blown away because I thought what I was doing was the will of God. I found out later that I was in good company that another pastor even though he had been on earth much longer had to learn this lesson as well. This pastor was none other than Moses the great man of God.

Exodus 18: Jethro was delighted to hear about all the good things the LORD had done for Israel in rescuing them from the hand of the Egyptians. *[10] He said, "Praise be to the LORD, who rescued you from the hand of the Egyptians and of Pharaoh, and who rescued the people from the hand of the Egyptians.* ¹¹ *Now I know that the* LORD *is greater than all other gods, for he did this to those who had treated Israel arrogantly."* ¹² *Then Jethro, Moses' father-in-law, brought a burnt offering and other sacrifices to God, and Aaron came with all the Elders of Israel to eat a meal with Moses' father-in-law in the presence of God.*

¹³ *The next day Moses took his seat to serve as judge for the people, and they stood around him from morning till evening.* ¹⁴ *When his father-in-law saw all that Moses was doing for the people, he said, "What is this you are doing for the people? Why do you alone sit as judge, while all these people stand around you from morning till evening?"*

¹⁵ *Moses answered him, "Because the people come to me to seek God's will.* ¹⁶ *Whenever they have a dispute, it is brought to me, and I decide between the parties and inform them of God's decrees and instructions."*

¹⁷ *Moses' father-in-law replied, "What you are doing is not good.* ¹⁸ *You and these people who come to you will only wear yourselves out. The work is too heavy for you; you cannot handle it alone.* ¹⁹ *Listen now to me and I will give you some advice, and may God be with you. You must be the people's representative before God and bring* their disputes to him. ²⁰ *Teach them his decrees and instructions, and show them the way they are to live and how they are to behave.*

²¹ *But select capable men from all the people—men who fear God, trustworthy men who hate dishonest gain—and appoint them as officials over thousands, hundreds, fifties and tens.* ²² *Have them serve as judges for the people at all times, but have them bring every difficult case to you; the simple cases they can decide themselves. That will make your load lighter, because they will share it with you.* ²³ *If you do this and God so commands, you will be able to stand the strain, and all these people will go home satisfied."*

²⁴ *Moses listened to his father-in-law and did everything he said.* ²⁵ *He chose capable men from all Israel and made them leaders of the*

people, officials over thousands, hundreds, fifties and tens. ²⁶ They served as judges for the people at all times. The difficult cases they brought to Moses, but the simple ones they decided themselves".

Jethro, Moses father in-law was Moses Pastor Green. He helped Moses to live longer and accomplish more. Moses was over working and slowly killing himself. What was the lesson that was taught first to Moses and next to me? It was delegation, the art of working yourself out of a job. Delegation is something that is not always easy to do. You must give away a part of you into the hands of someone who might not see the importance of the task as well as you. Here is another thing that might happen is that they are now empowered to do you more damage. I was preaching in Venezuela, a young man heard me and latched on to me. He was ambitious and had problems with his pastor. I counseled with him and told him it was important to make things right with his leader. He and his wife was working there; he was an American. He wanted to move to my city in the states and become a part of my ministry and did. He had worked with the embassy and had been influential in getting my Bishop's son a visa. Bishop was of course delighted and told me to make him an Elder. In obedience to my Bishop I did. This was completely against my leadership style; I believe in training before empowering and proved that I was right.

When you are a spiritual leader, you will discover that there will be things you will know before those you are leading will. So the leader has people around them that serve as counselors in the church. We were in a building project and I shared these things with the Elders of which he was one. He took this knowledge and used it against me as though I was deceptive and trying to hide something from the people. He told, as many as would listen and got enough to split the church and start his own. It was a very painful time in my life because not only did I love the people he seduced I loved him. I think I will share this to show you what I mean. I was given a call from his former pastor and told about a secret life he led there I had enough to hurt him and his family but refused to use what was given me.

We must not fight flesh with flesh. At this time, even family members were caught up in this. I know part of the problem was that he was not ready for this leadership role and I placed him there to soon. Some people want the stars without the scars. I shared this story not for your sympathy but to expose a trick of the enemy and not the one he used this young man to play on me but the one he used to keep us from building successful ministries because we feared these things happening to us. I talked about one man that caused me a lot of pain and if we are not careful people like him can cause you to become cynical and never employ people in God's work.

There was a book years back that said in the church there are three kinds of people, they are sheep, goats and wolves. No matter how great your ministry is we all have them. But if we focus on the wrong thing we will spend eighty percent of our time dealing with goats and wolves and forgetting the sheep.

Let me say he was not the only one who brought pain to my life there were others. Nevertheless, there were far more that brought blessings to my life. We had a team in The Fort Wayne church so many I would do an injustice to call and miss some ones name. They are like those in The Apostle Paul's life that stood out in their devotion and service. If I did not mention the late great Clifton Braithwaite, who stood far above the rest in his service to God and to me it would be a failure on my part. Mr. Reedy, Larry Dupree, Eugene and Myrtis Stephenson, Oliver and Millie Stephenson, David Hessing, Darlene Lundy, I had to mention these names but the list is much larger do not get offended if I missed your name you are remembered by me and more importantly God. So one-way to be worn down and to fall in sin; is to try to do this work alone or to focus only on your haters.

Use your time wisely

This is important because time has to be divided into many places. You need 1. God's presence 2. For your family and that include time for your wife alone and your children individual and collective time 3. The work of the ministry 4. You need some me time

God's presence

Psalm 91: *¹"Whoever dwells in the shelter of the Most High will rest in the shadow of the Almighty.[a] ² I will say of the LORD, "He is my refuge and my fortress, my God, in whom I trust."³ Surely he will save you from the fowler's snare and from the deadly pestilence.⁴ He will cover you with his feathers, and under his wings you will find refuge; his faithfulness will be your shield and rampart. ⁵ You will not fear the terror of night, nor the arrow that flies by day,⁶ nor the pestilence that stalks in the darkness, nor the plague that destroys at midday.⁷ A thousand may fall at your side, ten thousand at your right hand, but it will not come near you.⁸ You will only observe with your eyes and see the punishment of the wicked.⁹ If you say, "The LORD is my refuge," and you make the Most High your dwelling,¹⁰ no harm will overtake you, no disaster will come near your tent. ¹¹ For he will command his angels concerning you to guard you in all your ways;¹² they will lift you up in their hands, so that you will not strike your foot against a stone.¹³ You will tread on the lion and the cobra; you will trample the great lion and the serpent.¹⁴ "Because he[b] loves me," says the LORD, "I will rescue him; I will protect him, for he acknowledges my name.¹⁵ He will call on me, and I will answer him; I will be with him in trouble, I will deliver him and honor him. ¹⁶ With long life I will satisfy him and show him my salvation."*

Time in God's presence brings:

- God is a place of rest even in the middle of a storm

- A place of protection from your greatest haters

- Shows you how to get over and around traps the

enemy sets for you

- He is a remover of fear when facing danger, if you never have read Foxes book of martyrs I recommend you read it. When you see what God brought others through it will build your faith

- From his presence you will watch others fall but it will not come near you

- It is where harm cannot work

- Angels are given assignment concerning you

- Things that destroy others you, will declare cannot touch you

- His presence will rescue you when you wander out

- You will walk to success over your greatest enemies

- A place of assured answer to prayer

- A place of honor

- A place of longevity and satisfaction

- Where you see and learn his ways

So I believe with just this and there is so much more, you will find the time to stay in God's presence.

How do I stay in his presence?

- Read and study his word- Faith comes by hearing and hearing by the word of God.

- Prayer time - that is to commune with God - You must spend time with God every day. I do not always stop, go into a room, get on my knees, close my eyes and spend hours praying. I see him as a person and I talk to him all the time. He is an ever presence help in a time of need.

- Attend church services as often as they have them. When I first got saved I was going to Bible College twenty hours a week, youth meetings on Monday Wednesday and Friday, church Bible study on Thursday, prayer meeting on Saturday, church services Sunday morning and evening and would sometimes go and sit in choir rehearsal on Tuesday even though I was not a part. To combat the entire world I had just left I needed God's presence.

- Fellowship with other believers outside of church- some of my most precious moments were in the presence of other believers.

- Have a mentor- This is only a few of the people that help me in my journey, first even though I was not saved I must give thanks to Willie and Erma Bolden my parents who put the foundation under me. Church wasn't a choice in their home it was an obligation that you would fulfill or find you somewhere else to stay. The next group of people the help shape my life was Pastor John Lloyd having the vision to open a youth group that really worked, Thousands of people were saved at the Adam's Apple in Fort Wayne, Indiana. Another man I must mention I do not even remember his name, it reminds me of something Dr. Maya Angelo said "you may forget what someone did or said but you want forget how they made you feel" this brother would leave the suburbs and come in the hood and spend time mentoring me. There was of course Dr. Paul E. Paino, a prince of preachers. I give him credit for my ability to search study and preach the word of God. There was the late great Archbishop Benson Andrew

Idahosa, this man brought both pain and direction into my life I will focus on the direction. He was an enormously great man of faith. With the exception of a few that happen before meeting him most of the miracles in my life I attribute to his training. Neither time nor page would allow me to tell all the miracles I have seen.

- Next, you need to become a mentor.

Paul in these next scriptures encourages Timothy to do with others what he had done with him. 2 Timothy 2:1 "You then, my son, be strong in the grace that is in Christ Jesus. ² And the things you have heard me say in the presence of many witnesses entrust to reliable people who will also be qualified to teach others. ³ Join with me in suffering, like a good soldier of Christ Jesus. ⁴ No one serving as a soldier gets entangled in civilian affairs, but rather tries to please his commanding officer. ⁵ Similarly, anyone who competes as an athlete does not receive the victor's crown except by competing according to the rules. ⁶ The hardworking farmer should be the first to receive a share of the crops. ⁷ Reflect on what I am saying, for the Lord will give you insight into all this."

The ministry is given and learned. God calls us and put people in our lives to help us to keep moving forward. One of the greatest ways to grow is start to teach others.

Your family needs time

If you are a man or woman in ministry, you have responsibility to your family.

To the husband he says: Ephesians 5: ²⁵" Husbands, love your wives, just as Christ loved the church and gave himself up for her ²⁶ to make her holy, cleansing[b] her by the washing with water through the word, ²⁷ and to present her to himself as a radiant church, without stain or wrinkle or any other blemish, but holy and blameless. ²⁸ In this same way, husbands ought to love their wives as their own bodies. He who loves his wife loves himself. ²⁹ After all, no one ever hated their own body, but they feed and care for their body, just as Christ does the church—³⁰ for we are members of his body. ³¹ "For this reason a man will leave his father and mother and be united to his wife, and the two will become one flesh."[c] ³² This is a profound mystery—but I am talking about Christ and the church. ³³ However, each one of you also must love his wife as he loves himself, and the wife must respect her husband."

Ephesians 6: ⁴ *"And, ye fathers, provoke not your children to wrath: but bring them up in the nurture and admonition of the Lord."*

To the wife he says; Ephesians 5: ²² *"Wives, submit yourselves to your own husbands as you do to the Lord.²³ For the husband is the head of the wife as Christ is the head of the church, his body, of which he is the Savior. ²⁴ Now as the church submits to Christ, so also wives should submit to their husbands in everything."*

To both he tells them

Proverb 22: ⁶ *"Train up a child in the way he should go: and when he is old, he will not depart from it.*

To love nurture and learn submission takes time. Do not neglect and lose your family trying to build God's family, it is not his will".

Time for the ministry

Ephesians 4: *[11] "And he gave some, apostles; and some, prophets; and some, evangelists; and some, pastors and teachers; [12] For the perfecting of the saints, for the work of the ministry, for the edifying of the body of Christ: [13] Till we all come in the unity of the faith, and of the knowledge of the Son of God, unto a perfect man, unto the measure of the stature of the fullness of Christ:"*

It is important to know your responsibility as a leader or the ministry will eat up all your time. Paul tells us to help the saints grow to maturity, help them discover their work and to build up the body. If what you are doing is outside of these three things, you need to delegate it to others

Time for yourself

The devil and the people of God can put you on a guilt trip for taking time for yourself. I shared early about Moses over working. We as believers know that in the end times there will be a person call the anti-Christ as mention in the book of Daniel. Listen as Daniel described him and some of his goals. While doing that remembering in the New Testament Paul tells us that, his spirit is already here.

Daniel 7: [25] "And he shall speak great words against the Most High, and shall wear out the saints of the Most High, and think to change times and laws: and they shall be given into his hand until a time and times and the dividing of time."

You can see one of the things he plans to do is wear out the saints. If the devil will use this tactic tomorrow, he will use it today. Do not allow it to happen to you, take some time off, go on vacation, take days off doing the week and enjoy the abundant life God has given you.

Kingship Examination

- Attitude determines altitude
  1. True
  2. False
- Your mind is important according to Philippians four
  1. True
  2. False
- You are to guard your mind from fear
  1. True
  2. False
- Delegation is not important
  1. True
  2. False
- Things delegation can do
  1. Lighten burdens
  2. Place others in ministry
  3. Help the ministry grow
  4. All of the above
- Focusing on haters can drive you to sin
  1. True
  2. False
- Use of time is not important
  1. True
  2. False
- The work of the ministry takes priority over your family
  1. True
  2. False
- Satan desires if he cannot stop you to wear you out
  1. True
  2. False
- God wants you to enjoy an abundant life
  1. True
  2. False

King to do list

- Check your attitude by others analogy
- Read Philippians chapter four and Ephesians four and five
- Know and experience God's love
- Develop partners in ministry
- Focus on the lovers not the haters
- Budget your time
- Set romantic dates with your spouse
- Set time with your children

About the Author

Archbishop Willie Bolden

Education

Rosa A. Lott High School, Citronelle, Alabama

Christian Training Center Fort Wayne, Indiana

Taylor University, Fort Wayne, Indiana

IU/Purdue Fort Wayne, Indiana

Faith Theological Seminary, Tampa Florida- Master's and Doctoral Degrees.

Honorary Degrees: University of Benin, Benin City Nigeria, Benson Andrew Idahosa, University, Nigeria

Pastoral Experience

Founded Calvary Chapel church Inc. of Fort Wayne Indiana, with eight people. Built a twenty thousand square foot building, and the ministry grew to over two thousand in attendance. After the completion of the building in 1989 I placed a pastor there to oversee the ministry and moved to Tampa Florida to start another work. The ministry in Fort Wayne is still under my leadership and is called Lighthouse of Deliverance Cathedral.

Started Lighthouse Christian fellowship, now called Rehoboth in Tampa Florida. This ministry grew to over one thousand. In 2004, we purchased a fifty thousand square foot building for the worshipers. God began tugging on our heart and we had been praying about our new assignment and moved to Los Angeles Ca., where we built Rehoboth Faith Cathedral.

Ministerial Experience

Bishop Willie Bolden has traveled and ministered in most of the United States, ministering In Independent churches, Baptist, Methodist, Brethren, and Pentecostal just to name a few.

I have preached in the Bahamas, Jamaica, Trinidad and Tobago, Curacao, St. Martin, Port Rico, Guyana, Surinam, Kenya, Nigeria, England, France, Philippines. Culminating in over 40 years of ministerial experience, my work is not finished yet.

Awards

Outstanding Young Men of America, Accommodations from the Mayor of Fort Wayne for the work done in the inner city

In the United States Senate for the work done with inner city youth and gangs Was placed in the US Congressional records of 1990, especially for our work with youth,. Please find copies of some attached to this document.

Organization Bishop and President of a 501c3 non-profit Rehoboth Faith Cathedral registered in Florida and California.

Future Plans
- To establish another great church.

- To train and place pastors in the surrounding area and abroad in ministries.

- To establish a Bible College to aid in this work.

- To start a school to properly educate and prepare our children for the future.

- To form a Community Development Corporation, to assist in enhancing the lives of the underserved in our communities.

- Train and send out missionaries here and abroad.

- Continue to have conferences to aid those working in the church with the proper tools to get the job done.

- Train our youth to start and operate businesses

- We will focus a lot on the family, God has given

me and anointing that draws men, we will use it to train men how to properly take his role in the home.

- We will have marriage advancements, through marriage care workshops.

- Develop community forums to find how we can better serve them.

- Place a high value on our Christian children toward education without losing their testimony.

- Provide resources to assist persons with dealing with financial freedom and not debt.

- Encourage future planning, such as insurances to leave the next generation in a better place than we are, encouraging persons to include the church with ten percent of that plan.

- To continually write books.

Videos
http://www.youtube.com/watch?feature=player_detailpage&v=6Z2ccZqRTeQ

http://www.youtube.com/watch?feature=player_detailpage&v=AD1lCOkaGeI

http://www.youtube.com/watch?feature=player_detailpage&v=knwW1mMw4Co

http://www.youtube.com/watch?feature=player_detailpage&v=pT_9tS7B3-8

Personal

Bishop Willie Bolden was born in Mobile Alabama to Erma and Willie Bolden Jr. a Baptist Minister, was married to the late Pastor Glenda Bolden and has three wonderful children.

Contact Bishop Willie Bolden:

The five-fold ministry spoken of in Ephesians 4:11 embodies Archbishop Willie Bolden. He is an Apostle, Prophet, Evangelist, Pastor and Teacher.

As an Apostle: he will assist in the establishment of churches; he is anointed to build ministries.

As a Prophet: he gives spiritual encouragement, confirmation and correction when necessary.

As an Evangelist: he reaches out to the lost and reaches in to those in the body who need guidance

As a Pastor: He shepherds, builds, encourages and protects the sheep

As a Teacher: He trains, coaches, and mentors pastors, teachers, and others called into the ministry.

Archbishop Bolden is a gifted man of God who has dedicated his life to the restoration of the Kingdom of God. An author, professor and keynote speaker, Archbishop is available to assist those who desire to get all God has for them out of the ministry and out of lives.

Archbishop Willie Bolden, can be reached for seminars, workshops, and conferences via thewell@tampabay.org or by telephone at 310-729-9206.

Kingdom Alliance Ministry In'l (K.A.M.)

Email: bishopwilliebolden@aol.com

Blog: htp://www.bishopwilliebolden.com

www.ingramcontent.com/pod-product-compliance
Lightning Source LLC
Chambersburg PA
CBHW061308110426
42742CB00012BA/2103